ACCOUNTING AND QUICKBOOKS

2 in 1

Learn How to Use Small Business Bookkeeping Software for Beginners

KEVIN ELLIS

Table of Contents

ACCOUNTING

A Simple Guide to Financial and Managerial Accounting for Beginners

By Kevin Ellis

outlined in this book.

By reading this document, the reader agrees that under no circumstances is the author responsible for any losses, direct or indirect, which are incurred as a result of the use of information contained within this document, including, but not limited to, — errors, omissions, or inaccuracies.

INTRODUCTION

Thank you for purchasing, "Accounting: A Simple Guide to Financial and Managerial Accounting for Beginners." I hope you find this book informative and useful.

If you are looking for a guide that will help you gain a good understanding of accounting, this is the perfect book for you. It is designed to provide the reader with a basic but adequate understanding of financial and managerial accounting. You have to realize that accounting is a vast subject, and you cannot become an expert just by reading a single book. However, this book will provide you with enough information on accounting to help you understand everything you need as a beginner.

When you think of accounting, the first thing that comes to mind is crunching numbers. But an accountant does a lot more than that. Very few people recognize all that goes into accounting until they have involved in it themselves. This book will help you get familiar with all of this and more.

I am sure you are thinking, why is accounting important? Well, accounting involves a comprehensive and systematic record keeping of financial transactions related to any business. Accounting is important for various reasons. It is not just about keeping books or filing taxes. Even though these are two of the main tasks involved in it, there are many other facets involved in accounting too. In business, accounting will involve setting up accounting systems and preparing reports or statements related to all finances. There is a lot more than these things as well that you will soon learn. The point is, accounting is considered the language of business. It will help you understand how a business works and where it is thriving or declining. It allows you to ascertain what the financial position is for a business. Accounting reports allow management to determine what the business position is and what steps they need to take to improve the current position. Accounting is required for all business transactions. It will help to record, classify, and summarize of all the transactions. This enables proper analysis and creation of balance sheets, trial balance, and other financial documents.

Accounting plays an important role in decision making, controlling processes, and planning. The documents that are factored in all of this are created with the help of accounting. The methodical documenting involved in accounting will also prevent or reduce any incidence of theft or fraud in the business. Proper accounting will allow any business to run efficiently. It will enable effectiveness and accuracy in all activities. This will lead to better productivity and enable the management to make better decisions regarding the business.

In business, accounting will be involved in various functions. It is required for planning a budget. A proper budget will help the business run systematically. It will help to make strategies, save money, and also to prevent expenditure beyond what is specified in a budget. Records of financial statements in the business are required for a budget to be created. These documents will be available through accounting.

When you need a loan from a bank or any lender, you will be required to show your financial statements. These documents are only available if your business has a proper accounting system. This is how you can present any financial books to the bank. It will include records of profits, assets, or liabilities. Loans are only given out after scrutiny of such financial records.

Accounting takes care of the basic but crucial function of keeping records for a business. A business needs records to allow smooth running. Records have to be collected and organized well. They also have to be interpreted so the end-user can understand and make viable decisions based on these records.

The statements obtained through accounting will influence decision-making and provide information to investors in the business. Executives of a business cannot make sound decisions when they don't have access to accurate financial statements. If they don't have these documents, they will fail to achieve the objectives of their business. The lack of financial records will also have a negative impression on any investors in the business. Accounts will help them keep track of the progress or decline of any organization.

You can see that accounting is important in many different ways, and probably more than you previously expected.

Since this book is specifically aimed at providing information on financial and managerial accounting, let us get a basic introduction to them as well.

What is financial accounting? Financial accounting involves summarizing, analyzing, and reporting financial transactions that are related to a particular business. It is focused on providing useful information for the benefit of external users.

What is managerial accounting? Managerial accounting is concerned with accounting information that managers can use to help them in making better decisions so they can improve their management of the company's operations. It is focused on internal decision making, unlike financial accounting.

The book will cover a lot of topics, including:

- The accounting equation

- GAAP and IFRS
- Financial accounting
- Managerial accounting
- Financial statements
- Recording statements

All of these topics will be covered in detail to help you understand better. So, if you are ready, let us get started without further ado!

CHAPTER ONE

INTRODUCTION TO THE ACCOUNTING EQUATION

If you want to be an expert in the field of accounting, you have to familiarize yourself with the accounting equation. The double-entry accounting system uses the accounting equation as its basis. A company's balance sheet will display the accounting equation such that the sum of shareholders equity and the company's liabilities will be equal to the total assets of the company. It will ensure that the balance sheet of a company remains balanced based on this double-entry system. Every entry that is made on the debit side will have a corresponding entry made on the credit side.

The accounting equation formula is as follows for sole proprietorship:

Total Assets=Liabilities + Owner's Equity.

For a corporation, the formula will be:

Total assets=Liabilities + Stockholder's equity.

Calculation of the equation

- The accounting equation forms the basis of the balance sheet.
- The total number of assets if a company has to be located on the balance sheet for a period.
- All the liabilities have to be calculated and totaled under a separate listing on the same balance sheet.
- The total shareholder's equity has to be located and totaled. This has to be added to the total of the liabilities.
- The total assets will have to equal the sum of the liabilities and equity.
- The points to remember are:
- The accounting equation is the foundation of the double-entry system.
- The balance sheet of a company will show that the total assets of a company are equal to the sum of its liabilities and shareholder's equity.
- The assets are any of the valuable resources that the company owns.
- The liabilities are any obligations held by the company.
- The shareholder's equity and liabilities will represent how the company's assets are financed.
- It will be a liability if financing is done through debt. If financing is down by issuing equity

shares, it will be displayed as shareholders equity.

What is an Asset?

Any resources or a property possessed by an entity that not only has a certain monetary value but will also provide some form of economic benefit is referred to as an asset. An asset not only provides some benefit to a business but also helps improve its value. So, anything that a business owns is referred to as an asset. Assets are classified according to their liquidity, their use by a business, or the physical existence. Assets will include any cash or cash equivalents and liquid assets. This may consist of treasury bills or certificates of deposits. The amount of money that is owed by the customers to the company for product sales or services is known as account receivables. Assets will also include inventory.

Anything that the company owns will be considered an asset. This includes land, buildings, inventory, receivable accounts, cash, investments, and equipment.

Examples of assets include:

- Buildings
- Prepaid insurance

- Petty cash
- Cash
- Inventory
- Land improvements
- Equipment
- Goodwill
- Temporary investments
- Accounts receivable
- Asset Accounts will usually have debit balances.

Asset accounts with credit balances are Contra assets. Such contra asset accounts include:

- Accumulated depletion
- Accumulated depreciation buildings
- Accumulated depreciation equipment
- Allowance for doubtful accounts

In balance sheets, assets will be classified in a certain way. This means that the assets will be put under distinct categories or groupings. Accounts use this classification to bring more order to the balance sheet.

Assets will be classified in the following way on a balance sheet:

- Current assets
- Investments
- Property, plant, and equipment

- Intangible assets
- Other assets

Classification of assets

Assets can be classified according to their liquidity. Liquidity refers to the ability of an asset being converted into cash. Based on the liquidity, assets are classified into current assets or fixed assets. Any asset which can be readily converted into cash like inventory, short-term investments, stock, bank balances, bills receivable, or prepaid expenses will be classified as current assets. Any short-term asset will be referred to as a current asset. These assets are also referred to as liquid assets. Any asset, which cannot be readily converted into cash and this of a fixed nature, are referred to as fixed assets. Before these assets can be converted into cash, they usually have an extensive procedure for their sale. Examples of fixed assets include machinery and equipment, land and building, furniture and fixtures, and so on. Fixed assets are also known as long-term assets, hard assets, or even current assets. Fixed assets are subject to depreciation, whereas current assets aren't. Depreciation refers to the decrease in the value of an asset.

Assets can also be classified according to their physical existence. The two classifications of assets, according to their physical existence, are tangible assets and intangible assets. Any assets, which you can touch, feel, and see are referred to as tangible assets. All fixed assets are tangible assets. Also, there are certain current assets like cash or inventory, which can be considered to be as tangible assets. Any asset, which you cannot physically touch, see, or feel are known as intangible assets. The goodwill of a company, brand value, or trademark is intangible assets. Even if they don't have a physical existence, these assets influence the value of a business.

An asset can also be classified based on its use by the business. According to this classification, there are two types of assets, and they are operating assets or non-operating assets. Any asset that is used for day-to-day operations in business is referred to as an operating asset. All the assets that business users to produce the products or services it offers are referred to as operating assets. Examples of operating assets include bank balance, cash balance, inventory, plant apartment, and so on. Any assets that don't fall under the previous category are referred to as a non-operating asset. A business also has certain assets, which it doesn't use with day-to-day operations. These assets are, however, important for meeting its current and future needs. Examples of non-operating assets include any real estate property or excess cash reserves that are reduced for operational purposes.

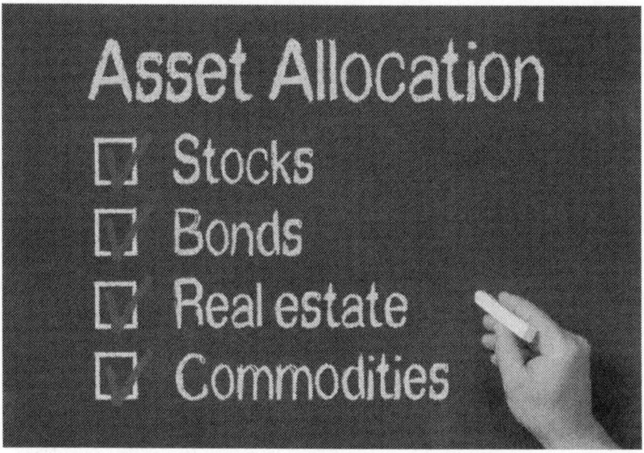

What is a Liability?

Liabilities comprise of what the company will usually owe others or have to pay so they can continue running. These are the obligations of the company. Liabilities include debt, rent, utilities, wages, taxes, salaries, loans, etc.

A liability can be viewed in two ways:

- It is viewed as claims by creditors against the assets of the company
- It is viewed as a source of the assets of the company.

Liabilities will also include any advance money that is received for further services. This amount revives will be received as asset cash but has not been earned yet.

This is why the company will defer to revenue reporting and report it as a liability instead. It will be marked under customer deposits or unearned revenue.

The following are examples of liability accounts in the balance sheet of a company:

- Accounts payable
- Interest payable
- Notes payable
- Wages payable
- Income taxes payable
- Customer deposits
- Salaries payable
- Other accrued expenses payable
- Lawsuits payable
- Unearned revenue
- Bonds payable
- Warranty liability

These liability accounts will have credit balances.

A liability account with a debit balance is a contra liability. If there is a debit balance in a liability account, it is contrary to the usual credit balance of the liability account.

Contra liability account examples include:

- Debt issue costs

- Bond issue costs
- Discount on notes payable
- Discount on bonds payable
- Liabilities classification

On the balance sheet, liability accounts and contra liability accounts will usually be classified. They will be put into distinct categories or classifications in the following order:

- Current liabilities
- Long term liabilities
- Commitments

The commitments of the company may be legally binding, but they will not be considered as a liability until some goods or services are received. Such commitments may include signing contracts for future services. If a commitment is of a significant amount, it has to be disclosed in the notes on the balance sheet.

Form vs. substance

When a certain asset is leased, it may appear like rental of it on the surface. However, in substance, it can be part of a binding agreement for purchasing the asset and financing it through monthly payouts. It is important for accounts to look past the visible form and to focus on the actual substance of a transaction. In substance, if a lease is an agreement for purchasing an asset and creating a note payable, the asset and liability have to be reported in the balance sheet and accounts.

Contingent liabilities

The following are three contingent liabilities examples:

- The warranty for the products of a company
- Guarantee of the loan of another party
- Lawsuits that are filed against the company

Such contingent liabilities will be potential liabilities because they will be dependent on future events that may or may not occur, and therefore, they may or may not turn into an actual liability.

For instance, take the case of a company being sued by a former employee for $200000 in wrongful termination. In this case, do you think the $200000 is a liability for the company? This would depend on two things. It is not a liability if the company has proper reasons and was justified in the termination of the employee. In such a case, the lawsuit will be frivolous. However, if the company had actually acted improperly and the employee was wrongfully terminated, there will be an income statement loss and thus a balance sheet liability.

Accounting rules for such liabilities exist. According to these rules, in case of a probable contingent loss and if the loss amount can be estimated, liability has to be recorded in the balance sheet with a loss being recorded in the income statement. In case of a remote contingent loss, liability or loss does not have to be recorded. It will not have to be included in the financial statements. In case the contingent loss is somewhere between these two conditions, it should be disclosed as a note in the financial statement.

Current vs. Long term liabilities

In case a company has a loan payable that has monthly payments due for several years, the principal amount that is due in the next twelve months has to be reported as a current liability in the balance sheet. The rest has to be reported under long-term liabilities. The interest of the loan pertaining to the future does not have to be recorded, the unpaid interest until the date of that balance sheet is the only liability recorded.

Notes to financial statements

You may have noticed how we mentioned notes repeatedly above. The notes to the financial statement can be very revealing and provide important information. These notes should be given special attention while going through the balance sheet of a company.

What is a Stockholders' Equity?

The total assets of a company minus its total liabilities are what will comprise of stockholder's equity. It represents the money that would be returned to all the stockholders in case the company assets were liquidated after debts were paid off. Stockholders equity includes retained earnings, and these are equal to the net earning percentage that the shareholders did not receive as dividends. These retained earnings are like savings because they arena total cumulative profit kept aside for future use.

The stockholder's equity will report how much was invested by owners into the company as well as the net income of the company that was withdrawn or distributed.

If you rearrange the accounting equation, you will get the following:

Owner's equity=Assets-Liabilities

Owner's equity will be marked on the balance sheet of a sole proprietorship company. In the case of a corporation, it will be marked as stockholder's equity.

Stockholders equity accounts will include:

- Common stock
- Preferred stock
- Retained earnings
- Accumulated other comprehensive income
- Paid-in capital in excess of par value
- Paid in capital from treasury stock and so on.

Owner's equity, as well as stockholder's equity, will have credit balances.

A contra owner's equity account is an owner's equity account, which has a debit balance. A debit balance is contrary to an owner's equity account because it usually has a credit balance.

In a corporatism balance sheet, the stockholder's equity section is:

- Treasury stock
- Retained earnings
- Paid in capital
- Accumulated other comprehensive income

Owner's equity vs. the company's market value

Asset amounts will report the cost of assets when the transaction takes place. This means that they won't reflect current market values that are fair. Since the fair market value of these assets is not reported, the owner's equity will not indicate the fair market value of that company.

Owner's equity and Temporary accounts

Income statement accounts include revenues, expenses, gains, and losses. Revenue and gain will cause an increase in owner's equity. The owner's equity will decrease expenses and losses. Assets will increase when a company performs a device so the owner's equity will also increase at the end of that accounting year when the device revenues account is being closed.

Accounting Must Balance

Accurate record keeping in the company will ensure that there is always a balance in the accounting equation. This means that the left side will always equal the right side. The accounting balance will be maintained because at least two accounts will be affected by a single transaction. For instance, take a scenario where a company takes a loan from a bank. In this case, the assets of the company increase, and so will the liabilities. It will be in the same amount on both sides. When inventory is purchased with cash, there will be an increase in one asset while another will decrease. The accounting system is called the double entry system because every transaction affects two or more accounts. All these transactions are tracked by keeping records in the general ledger of the company. Every account in this ledger will be designated accordingly - asset, revenue, liability, owner's equity, gain, loss, or expense.

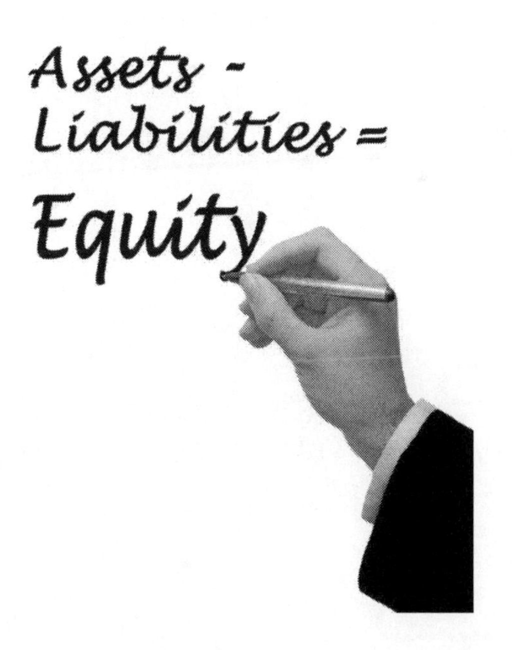

CHAPTER TWO

UNDERSTANDING GAAP

What is GAAP?

The full form of GAAP is Generally Accepted Accounting Principles. A common compilation of agreed accounting principles, methods, and standards that industry and their employees must obey while submitting the financial statements are referred to as generally accepted accounting principles.

Many companies mainly use GAAP for the following purposes:

- Organize all the financial information to accounting records.
- Collecting the accounting records and making a financial statement.
- Providing few supporting documents.

GAAP usually requires the company to maintain a minimum level of consistency in their financial statements, mainly for the investors to make their work of analyzing and getting useful information about the company easier and faster. GAAP also helps to compare the financial statements of different companies.

The following are the main aim of GAAP:

1. Principle of regularity

As GAAP rules and regulations are set as a standard, the accountant has to stick to it.

2. Principle of consistency

Accountants have to be consistent and apply the same rules and regulations in the entire process to avoid mistakes and discrepancies. The accountants have to mention and explain everything, and even if there's a minute change, they have to reason it out.

3. Principle of sincerity

The accountant tries her/his best to represent an exact condition of a company's financial condition.

4. Principle of the permanence of methods

The methods and techniques used in financial reporting have to be followed consistently.

5. Principle of non-compensation

Not only the positives but also the negatives have to be mentioned with clear details and without any expectations of debt compensation.

6. Principle of prudence

Focusing mainly on financial data representation with clear facts.

7. Principle of continuity

It should be assumed that the company is still running while calculating financial values.

8. Principle of periodicity

Everything entered should be classified into their relevant timelines.

9. Principle of materiality

The accountants should mention every minute detail in financial reports.

10. Principle of utmost good faith

It says everyone involved must maintain transactions genuinely.

GAAP includes the following:

- Financial statement presentation
- Properties
- Liabilities
- Equity
- Revenue
- Expenditures
- Business combination
- Derivatives and hedging

- Fair value
- Foreign currency
- Leases
- Nonmonetary transactions
- Subsequent events
- Industry-specific accounting like airlines, healthcare, and other activities.

These industries specified accounting in GAAP might be different in transactions than the others.

GAAP vs. IFRS

GAAP is mainly followed in the United States of American companies and is set by the financial accounting standards board (FASB). In other parts of the world, instead of GAAP, International Financial Reporting Standards (IFRS) are used and are issued by the international accounting standards board (IASB).

Since 2002, both the IASB and FASB have been working hard to merge GAAP and IFRS. As a result of this hard work, in 2007, the SEC had removed the requirement of a non-US company in the USA to comply with their financial statements with GAAP if it is already reconciled with IFRS. Before this, a non-US company in the USA had to comply with their financial documents with GAAP for trading in US transactions.

So, following are the differences between GAAP and IFRS accounting:

Locally vs. Globally

As mentioned, IFRS accounting is used in more than 110 countries and is globally accepted whereas GAAP is used only in America and has its own rules and regulations making it more difficult for American companies to do business outside.

Rules vs. Principles

One of the main differences between GAAP and IFRS accounting is the technique used in the accounting process. GAAP is strictly based on rules, and IFRS is more about overall patterns and is based on principle. As GAAP sticks on rules, everything is mostly clear so interpretation and exceptions are uncommon whereas in IFRS, even though accounts are the same, as it's based on principle, there can be different interpretations.

Inventory methods

In the GAAP method, they permit the Last In, First Out (LIFO) method for inventory estimates, whereas, in IFRS, a LIFO method is not allowed. LIFO method cannot be reliable as it's not accurate with inventory flow.

Inventory reversal

Not only do they have different tracking inventory methods. GAAP and IFRS accounting have a different policy in inventory write-down reversal. Whenever there's an increase on the market value of an asset, GAAP doesn't allow in reversing the inventory write-down, which reflects that GAAP is very careful with inventory reversal and doesn't implicate the changes on the market, whereas in IFRS the company can reverse the inventory write-down.

Developmental costs

The developmental cost of a company can be counted as an investment as long as they meet certain requirements on the company in IFRS. But in GAAP, the developmental cost would be considered as expenditure the same year and not as an investment.

Intangible assets

Research and development or advertising costs come under intangible assets. So, in IFRS, since they are principle-based accounting, they are very considerate about intangible assets and see if the assets can be beneficial in the future to the company. But GAAP considers intangible assets to be fair market value and nothing beyond.

Income statements

In GAAP, unusual or extraordinary items are segregated and mentioned below the net income portion of the income statement whereas in IFRS; these are not separated and included in the income statement.

Classification of liabilities

In GAAP, the debts of the company are separated into two sections. One is the current liability in which the company will be able to pay a certain amount at a certain period of time, and the other is the noncurrent liability where the company cannot pay the amount in that period of time. In IFRS, they don't have any differentiation, and all debts are put in one balance sheet.

Fixed assets

Fixed assets are the properties, furniture, and equipment of a company. So, in GAAP accounting, they value the assets using the cost of the model when bought minus the damage, repairing, and maintenance is done till date. Whereas in IFRS, they consider the cost of the asset by checking the cost in current time minus the damage, repairing, and maintenance done till date and is called the revaluation model.

Quality characteristics

Out of all, this is one of the main differences between GAAP and IFRS. GAAP functions on the hierarchy of characteristics like relevance, reliability, comparability, and understandability, to make the correct decision based on user-specific circumstances. IFRS also works similarly just for the fact that it doesn't decide based on user-specific circumstances of an individual.

Compliance

In accounting, a company's financial accounts and reports should be managed according to the federal laws and regulations, and it is called Compliance.

A company is bound to share every single minute detail to its shareholders and the regulatory authorities such as the Securities and Exchange Commission (SEC). It's very important for the procedures to be done correctly for recording, verifying, and reporting the total asset value of a company, liabilities, debts, and expenses.

In 2002, the Sarbanes-Oxley Act was applied as several scandals in corporate accounting were found. The act set a new standard s in accounting and internal auditing of these companies. The Sarbanes-Oxley Act has 11 titles, which explain the accounting and financial reporting compliance requirements.

Title 1: Public Company Accounting Oversight Board (PCAOB)

PCAOB was then established as a public agency whose function was to regulate, set policies and discipline accounting firms that used to provide auditing services for public traded companies.

Title 2: Auditor Independence

Before Sarbanes-Oxley came into action. All the auditing companies that were monitoring the accounting work of public companies were regulating on its own. Not only that, but also these companies were also consulting for the companies they were supposed to audit for. So, to avoid all these, this title was established to standardize the external auditor independence, which included auditor approval requirements, partner rotation, and reporting requirements.

Title 3: Corporate Responsibility

The above title specifically mentioned that the senior executives in the company were solely responsible for completing and submitting the financial reports of the company without any errors or mistakes. For example, the responsibility of certifying and approving the financial report contents was given to the corporations' senior-most officers like the CEO and the CFO.

Title 4: Enhanced Financial Disclosure

This title established some additional requirements for the transaction of the company's finance in various fields such as the stock transactions of corporate officers or off-balance sheet transactions. For compliance assurance of financial reports and disclosure, internal controls were also employed.

Title 5: Analyst Conflicts of Interest

Most of the primary investors of company's share had lost their trust in security analysts, so in order to restore their lost trust, this title was established in which the security analysts had to follow the code of conduct where they had to disclose any minute details of even small conflicts.

Title 6: Commission Resources and Authority

This title, like the previous one, was meant to show the security professionals work clearly for the restoration of investor's trust and confidence. It also allows the SEC's authority to either warn or exempt analysts from practicing.

Title 7: Studies and Reports

This title was beneficial as the Comptroller General and the SEC were asked to research and submit the report of their studies. The research included the impact of credit rating agencies on the securities market, the effects of consolidating the accounting firms, and involvement of investment banks in the accounting scandals of Enron, Global Crossing, and others.

Title 8: Corporate and Criminal Fraud Accountability

This title had set specific penalties for those who try to fraud the compliance investigations, and the 'whistle-blowers' were also given protection. This title is also called the Corporate and Criminal Fraud Act of 2002.

Title 9: White Collar Crime Penalty Enhancement

This title stated that the penalties for white-collar crimes and conspiracies would be more severe. This title stated that the corporate officers would be facing severe criminal charges if they fail to submit and get their financial reports certified. This title is also called as the White-Collar Crime Penalty Enhancement Act of 2002.

Title 10: Corporate Tax Returns

This title states that the CEO is solely responsible for the signing of the company's tax return.

Title 11: Corporate Fraud Accountability

This title is also known as the Corporate Fraud Accountability Act of 2002. This title enforced the fraud in corporate organizations and tampering of the company's record to criminal charges. Not only did they revise the sentencing guidelines, but also gave the SEC full right to stop doubtful transactions (huge or very unusual) till they were fully investigated.

Due to these strict rules and regulations, many companies find it difficult to cope with. Though many of the companies have proved themselves to be eligible and honest, the tight rules and requirements have shown the company's weakness and incompetence in the accounting systems. So, some of the companies have improved the accounting and internal processes, while the other has hired outside accounting firms to handle the accounting compliance.

Types of Accounting

There are three types of accounting and they are financial accounting, cost accounting, and managerial accounting.

Financial accounting

Financial accounting is mainly concerned with the record keeping which is directed towards the preparation of financial statements like the income statement and balance sheet. There are three main purposes that financial accounting serves. The first is that it helps to record transactions which are not just related to the business but also affect it. Financial accounting also helps in the preparation of necessary accounts and financial statements as the wand by the statutes and concerned loss. It also helps the owners of a business understand whether the businesses growing or not over a period. Financial accounting is the accounting for expenses, revenues, assets, and the liabilities. This is often restricted to all the published financial reports and is in direct contrast to internal branches of accounting like cost accounting.

Cost accounting

As the name suggests, this is the process of accounting for cost. It's a systematic procedure to determine the unit cost of an output produced or any service rendered by business. The primary function of cost accounting is to a certain the cost of a product and to help the management control its cost. Cost accounting deals with the classification, allocation, recording, summarization, and the reporting of current as well as prospective cost. Financial accounting as well as cost accounting are associated with the accumulation and the presentation of information for serving the needs of a management as well as other interested parties.

Management accounting

Management of any organization is primarily concerned with the supply of information, which is useful for the management in decision-making and for the efficient running of the business. The main idea of Management accounting is profit maximization. Management accounting is the reproduction of the final accounts or statements in such a manner that it helps the management to make decisions and to control activities. Management accounting is the term which is used to describe the accounting systems, methods, and techniques which, coupled with special knowledge and ability, assess the management in its task of minimizing losses in maximizing the profits. Management accounting is essentially a combination of financial accounting along with cost accounting.

You will learn in detail about all these types of accounting in the subsequent chapters.

CHAPTER THREE

FINANCIAL ACCOUNTING

Financial accounting is one of the specialized branches of accounting. It is used for keeping track of the financial transactions of a company. There are standardized guidelines that are used for recording, summarizing, and presenting the transactions in a financial report or statement. This can be in the form of something like a balance sheet or an income statement. Such financial statements are issued by companies quite routinely under a schedule. These financial statements are considered external because of the fact that they can be accessed by people outside of that company. This includes owners, stockholders, or moneylenders. This information will be accessible to even more people if the stock of that company is publicly traded. In that case, the financial statements are likely to circulate around more and will reach the hands of customers, employees, competitors, analysts, etc. You have to know that the main purpose of financial accounting is not reporting a company's value. In fact, it is actually so that others have just enough information that will allow them to assess the company's value for themselves. Different people can use external financial statements in different ways. The common rules of financial accounting are called accounting standards or known as generally accepted accounting principles. You will learn more about this later in the book. The Financial Accounting Standards Board in the U.S. is responsible for developing the standards and principles for accounting. If the stock of a company is traded publicly, the company is compelled to comply with the SEC's reporting requirements. The book will cover all of this in more detail.

Accounting Principles

In the field of accounting, there are some basic rules and guidelines that govern it, and these general rules are known as basic accounting principles and guidelines. Some of the detailed complicated, and legalistic accounting rules and guidelines are completely based on these accounting principles. The basic accounting principles and guidelines are also used by the financial accounting standards board (FASB) to set their own detailed and comprehensive set of accounting rules and standards.

Generally accepted accounting principles (GAAP) is comprised of three important rules, and they are:

- The basic accounting principles and guidelines.

- Rules and standards that are set by the financial accounting standard board and accounting principle board (apt).
- Commonly accepted industry practices.

When a company is making its financial statements public, while preparing those financial statements, the company is supposed to follow the generally accepted accounting principles. Also, when a company's stock trading is done publicly, the federal law has to audit the company's financial statements using independent public accountants. It has to be proven by both the companies' accountants and the independent public accounts that the company's financial statements and the related notes on the statement were made following the generally accepted accounting principles (GAAP).

It is proven that generally accepted accounting principles are very beneficial as it standardizes and regulates accounting definition, assumptions, and procedures. We can make sure that a company's method of preparing its financial statement is consistent throughout the year using generally accepted accounting principles. Even though there might be some exceptions, it can be said assuredly while differentiating companies or the company's financial statistics to the statistics of the industry. Since the financial transactions have become very complex, accordingly generally accepted accounting principles have become complex.

Functions of Accounting

Every business engages in several transactions. It can become quite difficult to keep track of all these transactions, and this is where accounting steps in. Accounting helps to keep the systematic record of all the financial transactions conducted by the business. By maintaining letters and financial statements, it becomes easier to stay on top of the financial transactions. Accounting also helps to secure properties owned by the business. A business can reach insolvency if there is an unauthorized dissipation of assets. Accounting helps to create a system that protects the assets of a business from unwarranted or unjustified use. Accounting involves not only the keeping of records but also the maintaining of financial statements. Financial statements communicate important results about businesses operating capacity to interested parties like creditors, government officials, proprietors, investors, or even employees. Apart from this, and the accounting system also enables that a business meets all the legal requirements put on by the federal and the State governments. The various statements that a business needs to file like sales tax returns and income tax returns.

Advantages of Accounting

There are various advantages of accounting and have been mentioned in this section.
The books of accounts provide a detailed and systematic record of all the transactions of a business. It is not humanly possible for one person to remember all the transactions made by the business. So, accounting helps by keeping track of all the transactions related to the day-to-day operations of a business. Financial statements like profit and loss account, trading account, and the balance sheet help understand the performance of a business. Based on the concept of consistency, a business needs to follow the same rules of financial, maintaining its books of records. Since all the books of records are maintained according to the same principles, it makes it easier to compare them. So, you can compare the performance of the business by using its financial statements from the previous years and measuring it against the present year. It gives a bird's eye view of how well a business is doing. It also identifies the areas where the business is lacking.
The primary aim of any business is to on profits. So, most of the decisions made by the business owner of the management will be directed towards attaining this objective. Financial statements make it easier for the top management to make decisions about a business and its future. The systematic records help to ascertain whether certain aspects of the business are doing well

or not. It also helps to determine the answer certain important questions like what the selling price of the goods must be or decisions regarding the procurement of the necessary raw materials.

Maintaining the books of accounts is also quite helpful in legal matters. A record of all business transactions can be provided as satisfactory evidence in a court of law. Apart from this, financial transactions provide necessary information to all the interested parties like the creditors, investors, business owners, governments, and so on. When this information is provided to the interest that groups, it becomes easier for them to make any decisions related to the business. For instance, if the financial position of the business is favorable, then it will be easier for a business to attain loans from its creditors. Every business needs to pay certain taxes. Taxes can't be paid if there is no record of proper financial transactions by keeping track of all the expenses are transactions; it becomes easier for a business to pay its dues. Fashion statements also provide information, which is necessary to plan certain operations like fear, cash requirement of the business, production, and so on. It also helps to make business forecast too. The financial health of a business can be gauged based on its financial statements. Apart from this, it also helps with the valuation of a business.

Now that you are aware of the different benefits accounting offers and the purpose it serves learning about it will make more sense to you.

Interested Parties

There are various parties who require the accounting information of a business. The list of interested parties includes owners, investors, creditors, governments, management, employees, and even researchers.

Owners

Owners include the proprietors of a sole proprietorship, partners of a firm, and the legal owners of the company or its shareholders. The information provided by accounting records is quintessential for the owners. The owners offer business started with the aim of earning profits. So, they need to have information about the following to steer the business in the right direction.

- A systematic record of earnings,
- All the expenses incurred,
- Any profits earned or losses incurred,
- Amount of capital available,
- Nature and the net value of all the assets owned,

- The quantum of liabilities owed,
- The record of any amount due to suppliers, creditors, or others related to credit purchases,
- Any amount owed by customers or others to the business for the sales of goods or provision of services,
- Accounting information along with facts for filing necessary returns like sales tax returns, income tax returns, all whilst tax returns.

Only when all this information is available to the owners will they be able to make qualified decisions. A businessman might not be able to ascertain the necessary facts about the business if there is no proper system of accounting.

Management team

The management along with the ownership of a sole proprietorship lies with the proprietor himself. However, there are various organizations like body corporate or partnership firms wherein the management and the ownership are different. The management of such businesses as often interested in any information pertaining to the business. They need accounting information for setting targets for the future or the upcoming financial year, for measuring and evaluating the performance of the organization, and for identifying any areas where the business is falling short. Most of the information that they need is a financial nature and will be prepared from accounting records.

Creditors

Every business requires capital for its day-to-day operations. Most of it comes in the form of the capital invested and any loans taken. Creditors include all the parties that provide a business with the necessary goods, raw materials, services, and other financial resources by extending a line of credit or providing loans. Lending companies, financial institutions, banks, and suppliers are all included in the group of creditors. Before providing credit or loan, a creditor will need to determine whether the business is capable of repaying the loan or not. Accounting records, along with financial statements, will help determine the financial health of a business. The common things that a creditor looks for are the business's existing cash position, any outstanding debts, and the current and future earning ability of the business. All this information is provided by the financial records of the business.

Potential investors

An investor would need to carefully analyze the financial position of a business before investing his money in it. A prospective investor often requires a detailed report about the progress of the company, along with its future plans. They require data about the past and the present performance of a business along with any key decisions that will affect the growth of the business in the future. Only after they have all these facts can an investor make an investing decision.

Employees

Just like creditors, even employees need the information associated with the working of a business. Since their livelihood depends upon the performance of the business, they will be interested in understanding its financial health. Most of the labor unions need accounting information of a business to analyze the salary and come up with any fringe benefits.

Governments

Every business is a financial entity and is required to pay certain taxes. It needs to pay federal as well as sales taxes. Governments need a record of the financial statements of a business to ascertain whether a specific concern is paying all its dues or not.

Basic Accounting Principles and Guidelines

If we can understand the accounting principles, we can clearly understand generally accepted accounting principles as it is based on it. Following are the main accounting principles and guidelines.

Economic entity assumption

The accountant has to separate all of the business financial transactions of a sole proprietorship and his personal transactions. But if it is for legal purposes, the business financial transaction and personal transactions of a person is considered as an entity whereas, for accounting purposes, they are separate entities.

According to this concept, every business is supposed to be treated as an entity that is different from its creditors, owners, managers, and other parties. So, the proprietor of an organization or business will always be distinct from the business he controls or owns. In the books of accounts, all the transactions need to be recorded from the perspective of the business and not that of the owner. If the proprietor invests capital in his business, the said capital will be treated as a loan to the business and the owner is a creditor.

The accounting principle of business entity applies to different forms of business organizations. For instance, from a legal perspective, a body corporate is deemed to be a separate entity. While a sole proprietorship along with this business is considered to be a single entity. This perspective changes when it comes to accounting. In accounting, business is considered to be an entity by itself. This is one of the most basic accounting principles, which has been accepted across the world. So, only the transactions associated with the business will be recorded and reported in the books of accounts. Any of the proprietor's personal transactions will not be included. While preparing the books of accounts or the balance sheet, the proprietor's assets and liabilities will not be clubbed with those of the business. The income earned by the business will be different from the income earned by the proprietor.

Monetary unit assumption

All the economic activities are counted in U.S. dollars, and they record transactions that are expressed in U.S. dollars only.

Only all those events or transactions that can be expressed in monetary terms are included in the accounting. Any event that cannot be expressed in monetary terms is excluded even if it affects the earning capacity of an organization. For instance, the working conditions of a company, the sales policy of an enterprise, the capability of the management team, the quality of products produced by a company, will affect the earning capacity. However, all these factors cannot be included in accounting because they cannot be expressed in monetary terms. So, anything that cannot be expressed in dollars will not be included. This concept puts a serious restriction on what can and cannot be recorded. Even though it has certain limitations, this is one of the most important concepts of accounting. It helps to improve one's understanding of and organization's working. Let us assume that a business has a plot of land, 2 tons of raw material, 40 tables, hundred chairs, a cash balance of $7000, and so on. In the absence of this concept, it wouldn't have been possible to include all these assets in the books of accounts. However, if the plot is valued at $30,000, the raw material at $4000 and the furniture at $5000, then all these items can be included as assets in the books of accounts.

A major limitation of this concept is that it doesn't take into consideration the purchasing power of money. The purchasing power of money changes along with time. For instance, if a building was purchased at $20,000 in 1960 and another was purchased in 1974, the same amount. Even if the previous building is worth more now, it will still be accorded at $20,000 in the books of accounts. As the purchasing power of money increases or decreases along with inflation, the value of assets also changes over time. This concept ignores inflation.

Dual aspect concept

This principle is the basis of accountancy. Every business transaction that is recorded in the books of accounts will have a dual aspect. The three important terms of this concept are based on our assets, capital, and creditors. Different writers tend to define asset in different ways. However, a common point to all the definitions is that it is an expenditure for acquiring valuable resources, which benefit the future activities of business. Building, machinery, furniture, inventory, debtors, land, and bills receivable are some of the examples of assets. Without these assets no business can be niche related or sustained. The assets that are business will depend upon the kind of profits it wants to make, and the industries involved in.

No business can run without assets. Now, the question arises where these assets are opting. One source of assets is the capital invested in business. The proprietor of the owner of a business invests his funds in the business in the form of capital. The amount of assets that are business has to be equally proportional to the amount of capital that the investor has. In other words, it can be said that when the proprietor puts his money in the business, this transaction gives rise to two effects; the assets of the business increase and the claim of the proprietor is also recognized. Since the system of thinking gives rise to two aspects, it is known as the dual aspect concept of the double entry system. In this case, the above event can be easily expressed as capital = assets.

In case the capital contributed by the proprietor is insufficient for a business to take off, then the business can borrow from others. All those who lend money to the business or give it some credit facilities are known as creditors. When you from the point of view of a business, each of these events also gives rise to two effects. On one hand, the loan obtained by the business will increase its assets and on the other, the claim of the creditor will also increase in the business. To sum up all the points up until now, capital + liabilities = assets.

Time period assumption

The net income of a business can be measured by comparing its assets from the time of its commencement to the date of liquidation. Since accounting is based on the concept that the business will go on for an indefinite period of time, measuring income using the above principle is not prudent. It is impractical for a business to fade for prolonged periods traded mine its net income. This is where the concept of accounting period comes in. If a business tries to measure its income from its conception to liquidation, you cannot determine whether the business is doing good or bad. To calculate its profitability, it is quintessential bad financial statements from time to time. Only when the financial statements are prepared can any corrective actions be taken. For instance, if for one quarter, a business has sustained significant losses, then corrective measures cannot be implemented without financial statements.

This principle states that in a short period of time, the company's complex and ongoing business activities can be reported with accuracy, for example, the five months ended May 31, 2019, or the five weeks ended May 1. 2019. When the time period is shorter, the accountant needs to assume the relevant amount in that short period. Suppose, the tax bill of the property is issued on December 15 every year so, the amount in the income statement in December end 2018 is known but the income statement in three months ending on May 31, 2019, is unknown, so the accountant has to estimate the amount.

It is very important to mention the time interval in the heading of every income statement, stockholder's equity statements, and statement of cash flows. One cannot label December 31 in these income statements. The reader should know if it is one week ended

December 31, 2019, the month ended December 2019, three months ended December 2019, or the year ended December 2019.

Cost principle

For an accountant, the word 'cost' means the money spent on an object when it was bought, despite its purchase time. This is the reason that the amounts in the financial statements are called historical cost amounts. There are two assumptions upon which the cost concept is based. The first assumption is that all the records will be recorded in the books of accounts at the price for which they were acquired. The second assumption is that the same cost will be used for any subsequent accounting related to the said asset. Whenever an asset is acquired, its net value tends to change over time. However, this change in net assets value is not considered while using the cost concept. For instance, if a piece of equipment was purchased for $8000, then it will be reflected in the final accounts as $8000 even if the market value is $7500. When a balance sheet is prepared based on the cost concept, it will not usually include the fluctuations in the net value of an asset.

If a business doesn't pay anything to acquire an asset, it will not show up in the books of accounts. So, if the business has any goodwill, it cannot be shown in the books of accounts since the company hasn't paid a penny to acquire it — objectivity and feasibility either to concepts which guide accounting activity. However, the cost principle fails to consider relevance while preparing accounts. At times, it isn't objective to try and estimate the market value of every asset given the fluctuations. The cost concept makes it more feasible. This concept doesn't help investors or other users because it usually shows the historical cost of the asset and not the existing cost. By following this concept, and the accountant is sacrificing relevancy for obtaining better feasibility and objectivity.

The company's asset is not changed or altered in regard to inflation because of this principle. The general rule is that an asset's value will not be changed to show any type of value increase. This is why the asset amount will not show the money that a company will get if it sells the asset in current markets value. There is an exception in some investments in stocks and bonds that are traded in the stock market. So, we cannot find a company's long-term asset value in the company's financial statements. A third party can do this job.

Full disclosure principle

Certain information is a must for the investors or lenders to know. So, this information should be mentioned in the financial statements or the notes attached to the financial statements. This principle is the reason behind many pages of 'footnotes' attached with financial statements.

The concept of full disclosure primarily implies that the accounts of a company need to be prepared honestly. It doesn't mean that all information needs to be disclosed, but sufficient information that can influence the interest of proprietors along with creditors and investors need to be disclosed. For instance, if a business has any contingent liabilities, they need to be showcased in the financial statements in the form of a footnote. For example, if a company is in a lawsuit and owes a lot of money when the financial statement is prepared, it is not sure if the company will win the case or end up losing money to the lawsuit, it's not clear so the lawsuit will be clearly mentioned in the financial statement.

Going concern principle

The going concern concept has been defined by Kohler's dictionary for accounting, as the assumption that a final indefinite period. It is based on the assumption that a business is not going to be liquidated any time soon. Indefinite existence means that a specific organization or business will not be liquidated in the foreseeable future. This essentially means that the concerned business is going to be able to meet any of its financial concerns and goals. The concept of liquidation is based on this principle. Fixed asset will appreciate its value over time. For instance, if a piece of equipment is acquired by a business and its expected lifetime is five years, then the total cost of acquisition of such a machine will be asserted for a period of five years while calculating the business's income.

In this accounting principle, the accountant can assume whether the company is going to prosper and achieve its motives and goals or not. If the accountant feels that the financial statement of the company shows or signals its liquidation, the assessment has to be disclosed clearly. This principle allows the company to defer a few of the prepaid expenses until the upcoming accounting period.

Matching principle

The most important factor that ensures that a proprietor will stay interested in his business is his desire to earn profits. Therefore, it is but obvious that an accountant's primary focus must be to improve the techniques for measuring income. An accountant's job is not just to calculate the revenue earned but must also calculate the expenses that have been incurred. There are two aspects of the matching concept, and they are the revenue realization concept and the matching costs. The first step to applying the principle of matching is to determine the period within which the revenue is realized. Revenue can be realized on the basis of sales, cash, or production. If revenue is recognized on sales basis, income will be recorded only when a sale is complete. A sale is completed when assets have been transferred to the buyer in exchange for a payment. Only when cash has received upon the realization of a sale will it be recorded in the books of accounts when the cash concept is followed. Revenue will be realized only when the production is completed when a business follows the concept of production bases. According to the completion of the work, the costs involved will be determined. For instance, a contract assigned to a construction job might require two years are the completion of the project. At such times, the contractor has the option of calculating his revenue and earnings from the project based on a percentage of completion. The second aspect of the matching concept is the matching of cost. Whenever the income from the business operation is being calculated, the course that was incurred while earning the revenue needs to be included. So, certain costs like from the sale of capital assets, loss incurred due to an accident, and other causes even though not related to the regular business operations need to be included while calculating the revenue. Anything which leads to cash flow from the business must be included.

In this, the accounting principle, the accrual basis of accounting is applied. The matching principle states that expenses have to match with the revenues. For example, the commission expenses should be mentioned when sales were made, and not when commissions are paid. The employ wages should be reported when the employees are working and not when the wages are given. So, if a company is going to pay 1% of 2019 sales to their employees on January 15, 2020, it should be mentioned as an expense in 2019 and the amount unpaid in 2020 as a liability. Since the advertisements benefit cannot be confirmed, the ad expenditure is out in as an expense until the ad is running.

Revenue recognition principle

According to the revenue recognition concept, there are two things that must be considered. The first aspect is that a transaction will only be recognized whenever there is an inflow or outflow of funds. The second aspect is that revenue must be recognized at the point of sale while keeping consideration of any gains or losses that were incurred during the course of the transaction. According to revenue recognition concept, revenue can be realized by the business only when the goods or services produced by it are transferred to the customer either for some asset, cash or for some promise to pay the cash in future. This is closely related to the legal principle related to the transfer of any property. Revenue must be recognized only when the business actually sells something to the customer. For instance, if a business receives an order to supply goods in June in the month of March, then the sale will be realized only June. This concept is quite important because it prevents businesses from inflating their incomes or profits by recording any future sales. Transactions need to be recorded only when they are finalized, and the payment has been received.

This principle also follows the accrual basis of accounting and not cash basis of accounting. So, in this principle, revenue is considered right after the product is sold off or the service is performed, if the money is received is not taken into consideration. So, in this principle, a company can report almost $30000 revenue and still have $0 in their account in that month.

Suppose, if Vogue has agreed to post an ad for 3000$, Vogue can report $3000 right after signing the deal even if the money is transferred after 30 days. So, revenue and cash receipts should never be confused.

Materiality

It is the accountant's duty to make an objective distinction between transactions that can be considered to be material or immaterial. If an accountant fails to make this distinction, then the accounting process will be unnecessarily overburdened by several minute details that don't add any value.

According to the American Accounting Association materiality is defined as follows.

An item is considered to be material when there is a reason to believe that its presence or its knowledge will influence the decision of an investor or other interested parties. If anything can influence the judgment of a prudent man, then it is considered to be a material transaction. At times are certain unimportant items which are left out of financial statements are merged with other items. These items can be either shown as footnotes or in parentheses based on their importance. For instance, the amount of profit or loss shown in the profit and loss account can change because of a change in the business's accounting practice. Any change in the calculation of depreciation will influence the profit or loss incurred on the sale of the assets. If it is believed that this information will not influence and interested party's decision, then it doesn't have to be included in the business accounts. All such information must be disclosed, which can affect the decision of existing or potential investors.

Conservatism

The principle of conservatism is based on the idea of playing safe. While following this concept, a business takes into consideration all losses while understating any prospective profits. By following this concept, and the accountant will record all unfavorable events that can affect the value of an asset, owner's equity, and income. The least favorable effects are immediately recorded while leaving out any prospective profits. For instance, any provision that is made for doubtful debts or any discount given to debtors will be included by following this concept. Any provision created for fluctuations in the price of assets or investments like depreciation will be recorded during the following conservatism. Along with that, amortization of intangible assets will also be included. This concept is usually applied whenever that happens to be any uncertainty regarding an activity. An inherent uncertainty can be about incurring a loss, an estimated liability, or even the useful life of an asset. By following this concept, and the accountant has the option of choosing a conservative approach when there are two acceptable methods of accounting involved. Whenever there happens to be a possibility of incurring a loss of earning a profit, then the profits will be overlooked while the loss will be accounted for. By doing this, it enables a business to prepare itself any potential losses.

This conservatism principle helps the accountant when in a dilemma with two acceptable alternatives in mentioning an item. So, this principle allows the accountant to choose the option in which the end result will lead to less asset amount and/or less net income. This principle doesn't allow the accountants to be conservative. The accountants are supposed to be completely unbiased and practical.

So, this conservatism principle will allow accountants to mention down losses and not the gains. For example, if a company loses a case in a lawsuit, the accountants will mention it, but if it gains extra in the case, they are not going to mention it. However, this concept needs to be used cautiously. If this principle is used without any restrictions, it leads to the creation of secret reserves, which will be in direct contradiction of the full disclosure principle. The idea is to enable the business to fortify itself from any losses. So, it must not be misused to deceive other parties involved in the business.

Other Characteristics of Accounting Information

Following are the characteristics of accounting information when a professional accountant provides the accounting information:

- It should be reliable, verifiable, and objective.
- There should be consistency
- Accounting information should have comparability

Reliable, Verifiable, and Objective

Not only should a piece of accounting information follow all the above-mentioned accounting principles and guidelines, but should also be reliable, verifiable, and objective.

This concept means that all the accounting transactions must be evidenced and supported by business documents. The supporting documents include invoices, correspondence, and so on. The supporting documents provide the basis for making accounting entries and for verification of the same by auditors. The evidence of stands in the business transaction must be objective evidence. It essentially means that the evidence should support packs as they are without any bias toward either side. This concept forms the basis of auditing.

Suppose, if the mentioned says a land purchased 50 years ago at $ 60000, it looks more reliable, verifiable, and objective than the current price value of $ 400,000. If the original cost is given to many different accountants, all of them will come to one conclusion about the original cost based on the offer and acceptance, transfer tax and the documents. But if the current market price value is given to them, all of them will come out with a different end result. It therefore becomes unreliable, unverifiable, and not very objective.

Accounting principle has nodded to move away with the cost principle if the amounts are reliable, verifiable, and objective. For example, if a company has bought a stock, and the stock is currently traded in the stock exchange, the company has to show the current rate instead of the original bought value. The one limitation of this concept is that it isn't possible to verify every single entry that is made. Certain steps can be taken to ensure that all the data entered is true and fair, but 100% accuracy cannot be guaranteed when humans are involved.

Consistency

The accountants of the company have to be consistent in applying accounting principles, methods, and practices. Accounting practices, as well as concepts, need to be practiced consistently. If the management is to draw any important conclusions about the effectiveness of the business, there needs to be consistency. If the methods keep changing from one accounting period to another, it becomes difficult to compare the performance of the business. Consistency doesn't mean rigidity. New techniques of accounting can be introduced, but they need to be used consistently.

The principle of consistency comes in handy whenever there are various methods of accounting that can be used for a particular transaction. For instance, depreciation will be charged over the lifetime of a fixed asset. However, when it comes to calculating depreciation, there are several methods available. Businesses are free to charge depreciation according to any of these methods. If the business decides to charge depreciation according to the straight-line method and needs to ensure that the method of depreciation will be followed over the course of the life of an asset, if the method keeps changing from one accounting period to another, it will become very difficult to assert on the net value of the asset.

If a company has been using the FIFO cost flow assumption, the financial statement readers will expect the company to be using it. If the company switches to using the LIFO cost flow assumption, the accountant should mention it clearly in the financial statement.

Comparability

If it is in the same type of industry, investors, shareholders, and other users expect that the financial statement of one company can be compared to the financial statement of the other company. Comparability between different financial statements of many companies is one feature of Generally Accepted Accounting principles.

Financial Reporting

The disclosure of a company's performance in finance and other related information over a certain period of time to the management and external stakeholders like an investor, customer, and regulators is called financial reporting.

The financial reports are issues either quarterly or annually and consist of the following:

- Balance Sheet or Statement of Financial Position – this consist of a company's assets, liabilities, and owner's equity at a given time, which is usually the fiscal quarter or year.
- Income Statement or Profit and Loss Report – this consist of the income, expenses, and profits of a company over a certain period of time, usually the fiscal quarter or year. So, this comprises of the total sales and many expenses done during that given period of time.
- Statement of Changes in Equity or Statement of Retained Earnings – it mentions the equity changes of a company during the given time period usually the fiscal quarter or year.
- Cash Flow Statement – this consist of the cash flow activities in the company, which includes, operating, investing, and financing activities. These are called as sources and uses of cash.

These financial reports will be very detailed and complex in publicly held corporations. They usually add extensive footnotes, and along with that, they include a management discussion and analysis (MD&A). These footnotes provide detailed information about each item listed on the balance sheet, income statement, and cash flow statements. These notes also include the type of method used for preparing the accounting report.

The private and public companies have to follow generally accepted accounting guidelines (GAAP) while preparing their financial reports. U.S. companies have to report under the U.S. generally accepted accounting guidelines (GAAP), and the other international companies have to report under International Financial Reporting Standards (IFRS). When the accounting principles and guidelines are followed in accounting, it assures accuracy, consistency, and comparability in the financial report.

Cash Basis Accounting vs. Accrual Accounting

The main differentiating fact between cash and accrual accounting is the timing of the sales and purchases recorded in the accounts.

Cash basis accounting only records revenue and expenses only when the money is received in the account, whereas in accrual basis accounting, revenue is considered as soon as it is earned, and the expenses billed.

Cash basis accounting

In cash basis accounting, revenues are taken into consideration only when it is received, and the expenses are considered only when the bill is paid. This method of accounting does not consider the accounts that will be received or paid later.

Most of the small-scale businesses choose this method of accounting because it is very simple and easy to regulate. It is very easy to track when a transaction is done and if the money has been deposited or sent from a bank account. There is no need to keep track of the accounts that are to be received or paid.

This cash basis accounting method is also very beneficial in checking the company's current bank account balance at any given time and checks the resources of the money.

And since the transaction is not recorded until the money is in the bank account, the business income tax is not taxed unless it's in your bank account.

Accrual basis accounting

In this accrual basis accounting method, the revenues and expenses are noted and recorded immediately when they are earned or billed, regardless of whether the money is actually received or paid. For instance, a company will add the revenue right after completion of a project rather than waiting for the payment to be received. This method is used and followed more than the cash basis accounting method. Normally, all transactions are settled in cash but even if settlement of cash has not yet taken place, it is justified to include the transaction are the events related to the books of accounts. The accrual concept recognizes revenue when it is earned rather than when it is collected and recognizes expenses when assets or the benefits are used rather than when they are paid for. The financial statements might not reveal the true and fair view of the affairs of a business unit undersold the transactions are events related to a particular year are entered into the books of accounts. So, by following the accrual basis of accounting, this can be done.

This accrual basis accounting method provides a better view or sight of a company's income and expenses, so it gives better information about the company's future business conditions. Cash basis accounting cannot do this.

The main disadvantage of this accrual basis accounting is that the actual cash flow is not at all informed. So even though a company might be making a lot of money in accrual accounting but in reality, can be out of money in a bank account so it is very important to keep track of bank account or cash flow also the end result can be disappointing.

The effects of cash and accrual accounting

It is very important and moreover mandatory to know the difference between cash basis accounting and accrual basis accounting when you start a business. And also, you have to see the effects of each of these accounting methods.

These are the ways each cash and accrual basis accounting effects:

Suppose you do the following transactions in a month of business:

- Sent an invoice of $7000 for a web design project that was completed this month.
- Received $3000 for developing a website this month.
- Gave $300 in fees for a bill, which you got last month.
- Received $3000 from a client for a work given last month.

The effect on cash flow

If we use the cash basis accounting method, the total profit of this month will be $ 2700 ($3,000 income minus $300 fees).

If we use the accrual accounting method, the total profit of this month will be $4,000 ($7,000 income minus $3,000 developer fees).

The above example shows that the two different accounting methods can lead to different accounting of profits and cash flow. So, the choice of accounting method does make a huge difference.

The effect on taxes

Suppose we consider that the above-given example happened in between November and December 2018. One of the main differences between the two accounting methods is that they have a huge impact on the business tax depending on the time the income and expenses are recorded,

If we use cash basis accounting, the income is only recorded when the cash is received in the bank account, whereas if we use accrual basis accounting, it is recorded right after it is earned.

So, if we follow the accrual basis accounting, if the invoice for $7000 was confirmed on December 2018, it will be recorded as a transaction done in 2018 and pay income tax for it even if you receive the cash in January 2019.

Types of Accounts

An account is often referred to as the formal record of a specific type of transaction that is expressed in monetary terms. When it comes to the double-entry system, every transaction has a twofold effect. Therefore, there are two accounts that are involved. One account will be debited, whereas the other will be credited. For the purposes of accounting, every transaction made bad business can be classified into three categories.

- The transactions that are relating to individuals are persons.
- The transactions relating to property, possession, or assets.
- The transactions relating to incomes and other expenses.

Corresponding to the three categories of transactions that were mentioned above, the following three classes of accounts are prepared for recording all the business transactions.

- Personal accounts.

- Real or property accounts.
- Nominal accounts.

Now, let us look in detail about each of these three types of accounts. It is quintessential to learn about these accounts because the basic rules of debit and credit are based on it.

A personal account is used for recording any dealings of a trader or a business with other persons of forms. A separate account will be opened for each such person, performed for recording the transactions. The account of each person at the firms will be debited with any benefit such a person or firm receives and is credited with any benefit that such a person or firm provides. Personal accounts are further classified into the following.

Natural person's account

For instance, includes supplier's accounts, receiver's accounts, and proprietor's accounts.

Artificial person's accounts or body of person's accounts: For instance, any bank account, insurance company's accounts, government's account, and any limited company's account.

Representative personal accounts: Includes any account that's used for representing a particular person or persons. For instance, if a business cannot pay the salaries to its employees, then the account created in the books of the business would be Salaries Outstanding Account.

Real accounts

Real accounts are also referred to as property accounts, and the record any transactions related to property, assets and possessions of business. All those items, which are more or less permanent, are recorded in the real accounts. A separate account is maintained for each class of property or possession owned by the business such as stock of goods, equipment, furniture and fixtures, cash, machinery, and so on. In each of these accounts, the particular is related to that asset are maintained. It helps a business to identify the net value of each of its assets on a given date. Real accounts are classified into tangible real accounts and intangible real accounts. Tangible real accounts include all tangible assets like land, cash account, stock account, furniture account, building account, and so on. Intangible accounts include trademarks, patents rights, and goodwill accounts. These accounts include all such things that are difficult to touch in the physical sense but are capable of being measured and pecuniary value.

Nominal accounts

Fictitious accounts or nominal accounts are these accounts are used for defining the nature of transactions. These accounts are used for recording any losses or gains of a business. Here is an example to make things clear. If an employee gets his salary, and the agent gets his commission, a worker gets his wages; a lender gets interest on money, all dealings are made in cash. Cash is the real thing that exists, and salary, commission, interest, wages, and other terms are used for merely describing the nature of the transaction for which the cash was used. If nominal accounts didn't exist, it would become rather difficult to keep track of all essential business transactions.

Rules for Double-Entry

Now that you're aware of all the different types of accounts, it is time to learn about the double-entry system. The double entry system basically provides the rules of debit and credit. Every transaction has two aspects - an incoming aspect (debit) and an outgoing aspect (credit). The rules of the double-entry system are based on these two aspects. Since there are three types of accounts, there are three rules for recording all the transactions in the respective accounts.

Rules for personal account

The person account holders receive something from the business will be debited while the person's account who give something to the business will be credited. If ABC gives $2000 to the business, then it is said that ABC's account will be credited.

Rules for real account

All the assets that are acquired by the business will be debited, and all those that go are the business will be credited. For instance, if business purchases are building for $ 100,000 in cash, then the building's account will be debited, and the cash account will be credited.

Rules for expenses and incomes

All expenses and losses will be debited while all incomes and games will be credited. For instance, if the rent is paid by a business, then the rent account will be debited while the cash account will be credited.

CHAPTER FOUR

RECORDING TRANSACTIONS

When the transactions of a company are recorded in the general ledger accounts, it is called bookkeeping. This term is usually used to refer to any accounting task that is carried out before preparing the trial balance.

Different people will think of bookkeeping in different ways:

There are people who think of bookkeeping as accounting itself. They will assume that everything some keeping the company's books to preparing tax reports is included in bookkeeping.

There are those who see it as just recording transactions in a journal or diary. The amounts are then entering into the accounts in the ledger. This signifies the end of bookkeeping for them; a real accountant then handles the work.

Using computers and advanced accounting software has blurred the lines that differentiated bookkeeping and accounting. Even someone with basic training in bookkeeping can use accounting software. The software will automatically update general ledger accounts after the records are entered. After establishing the financial statement format, this software can generate financial statements too.

Bookkeeping is not a term that is used in larger corporations anymore. Such organizations usually have a whole department that is dedicated to accounting and staffed with well-trained accountants.

You have to understand the relationship of bookkeeping with accounting. There is some confusion over the distinction between bookkeeping and accounting. This is due in part to the fact that the two are related and that there is no universally accepted line, which demarcates them. Usually, bookkeeping is the art of maintaining or keeping the accounts in a prescribed manner. Accounts are maintained for registering for noting the facts of transactions in a clear and understandable manner. Most of the work related to bookkeeping is clerical in nature. Accounting is mainly concerned with the design of the system of records, preparation of reports based on the recorded data, and the interpretation of the report. Accountants often direct and review the work of keepers. Bookkeeping is an activity that is complementary to the process of accounting. Accounting develops information for providing answers to the following questions.

How good or bad is the financial condition of the business? Have the operations of the business of the whole resulted in a profit or loss? How have the different functions of the department performed? And how successful have been the results of individual activities of products? What are the likely results of new decisions to be made or old decisions that may be modified? In the light of the past results of operations, how must the business enterprise planned activities attain the expected results?

Accounting and bookkeeping will involve recording financial transactions of the company. These transactions are to be identified, approved, and sorted so that they can be retrieved when needed and presented in financial statements of the company.

The following are some examples of financial transactions of a consonant:

- Using cash to purchase supplies
- Using the credit to purchase merchandise
- Using credit for the sale of merchandise
- Rent for business office
- The wages and salaries of employees
- Buying equipment for office
- Borrowing from banks

All of these transactions will be sorted into accounts, and the amounts that are in each account will be reported in the financial statements of the company.

This may be in a summary form or in detail. There may be hundreds of accounts and an even greater number of transactions. This will allow more efficiency and information that will help to manage the business better.

Since there is sophisticated accounting software available now, it is impractical to use manual accounting for a business. A minimum amount of data entry is required for the software to do all the work for accounting. One of the most popularly used accounting software is QuickBooks.

Why are Debits and Credits Important?

The terms debit and credit have actually been used for hundreds of years and are not as modern as they might sound.

The double entry system will require every transaction to be recorded in two accounts. The first account will receive an entry of debit, and this entry will be done on the left side. The other account will receive an entry of credit, and this will be done on the right side. Initially, in double entry, it may be confusing to decide which account has to be debited and which account credited.

Debiting an account means making entries on the left side of that account. Crediting an account will mean making entries on the right side of that account. Abbreviation for debit is dr. and the abbreviation for credit is cr.

The following types of accounts are usually increased with debits:

- Dividends
- Assets
- Expenses
- Losses

The following account types are usually increased with credits:

- Gains
- Income
- Revenues
- Liabilities
- Stockholders equity

To decrease account on one side, opposite of what was done to increase will have to be done. If a debit increases an account, a credit can be used to decrease the account.

Journal Entries

The term journal entry comes from the fact that in manual accounting, business transactions are first recorded in journals.

The journal entries in the general journal of a company will contain the following information:

- The correct dates
- The account that will be debited
- The amount that will be debited
- The account that will be credited
- The amount that will be credited
- A short reference

Journal entries in the journal will be entered according to dates, and then they are entered in their appropriate accounts of the general ledger.

The journals are referred to as the book of verse or original entry. Since all transactions are first recorded in the journals before they are transferred to any of accounts. The journal provides a chronological order of all the transactions made by the business. It shows the date wage transaction along with the amount sought the accounts that have to be debited or credited. Journals also often provide a brief explanation of the transaction involved. Every business transaction can be recorded in a simple journal. A business deal can also record specific transactions in different books of accounts known as special journals. Special journals include Sales Journal for any credit sales, Purchases Journal for any credit purchases, Purchases Returns Journals, and so on. Journals are created on the basis of the double-entry system of accounting. So, every transaction made by the business has two effects. Let us look at a couple of transactions to get a better idea of how journal entries are made. For instance, ABC starts a business with $ 50,000, and the capital is in the form of cash. So, the journal entry for this transaction would be as follows.

Cash A/c Dr. --------------- $50,000

To ABC's A/c --------------- $50,000.

(Being money invested in the business)

If $4000 is paid as rent by the business, then the transaction will be recorded as follows.

Rent A/c Dr. --------------- $4,000

To Cash A/c --------------- $4,000.

(Being rent paid in cash)

In computerized accounting, business transactions will be recorded automatically into the general ledger. This is why journal entries are not written for most business transactions now.

However, despite using computerized accounting, some journal entries still have to be made. This includes the adjusting entries.

General Ledger

A general ledger will be a grouping of accounts that are used for sorting and storing information from the business transactions of a company. It will be organized as balance sheet accounts and income statement accounts. The balance sheet accounts will include equity, assets, and liabilities. The income statement accounts will include gains, losses, expenses, and revenues.

If you use the double-entry accounting system, every transaction made will affect two or more than two general ledger accounts. The debit amount of every transaction has to be equal to the credit amount. This is why the general ledger should have an equal number of debits and credits. When totaled, the account balances that are listed on trial balance should be equal.

In the case of manual accounting, general ledgers are usually books where there is a separate page kept for every account. A subsidiary ledger is used if a lot of information is required for an account. In computerized accounting, the general ledger will be in the form of an electronic file that has all the required accounts. This helps to facilitate electronic preparation of the financial statements of the company.

What is a general ledger account?

It is an account that is used for sorting, storing, and summarizing the transactions of a company. The accounts will be arranged in the general ledger. The balance sheet accounts come first, and then the income statement accounts.

Balance sheet accounts will usually be arranged like the following in a general ledger:

- Asset accounts, like inventory, accounts receivable, and cash.
- Liability accounts like customer deposits, notes payable, and accounts payable.
- Stockholders equity accounts like treasury stock and common stock.
- Income statement accounts will be arranged as:
- Operating revenue accounts, like sales fee revenues.
- Operating expense accounts like rent expense.
- Non-operating accounts like interest expense.

Subsidiary Ledgers

Subsidiary ledgers are often prepared in addition to a general ledger. These are used to record details related to accounts receivable along with Accounts Payable. If there are thousands of customers and numerous credit sales transactions can become quite cumbersome to record them in the general ledger under the heading accounts receivable. It becomes impossible to a certain quantum of the amount receivable from a specific buyer. It also becomes equally difficult to calculate the amount that is owed by a specific customer if the records are maintained only in a general ledger under the heading accounts payable. Instead of this system, a subsidiary ledger is maintained to specifically a certain the amount receivable from an individual director along with the amount that payable to an individual creditor. A group of accounts maintained in this fashion is known as subsidiary ledgers. When these ledgers maintained, it is not required to maintain a detailed account of the accounts receivable or payable on the general ledger. There are two types of common subsidiary ledgers maintained by any business- the accounts receivable subsidiary ledger and the Accounts Payable subsidiary ledger. The data in these ledgers maintained in alphabetical order. The data from subsidiary ledgers is briefly recorded in certain accounts of the general ledger, and they are known as the control ledgers. At the end of an accounting period, the total of each subsidiary ledger will be equal to the balance of every control account. For instance, the balance of accounts payable in the general ledger will be equal to the total balances of all the individual accounts maintained in the Accounts Payable subsidiary ledger.

Let us look at an example to understand this relationship.

X

Date	Account title Balance	Ref	Debit	Credit
2019		$	$	$
Feb 2	Sales	12,000		12,000
Feb 15	Cash		8,000	4,000

Y

Date	Account title Balance	Ref	Debit	Credit
2019		$	$	$
Feb 12	Sales	6,000		6,000
Feb 21	Cash		6,000	Nil

Z

Date	Account title Balance	Ref	Debit	Credit
2019		$	$	$

Feb 20	Sales	6,000		6,000
Feb 25	Cash		2,000	4,000

General Ledger- Accounts Receivable

Date	Account title Balance	Ref	Debit	Credit
2019		$	$	$
Feb 28	Sales	24,000		24,000
Feb 28	Cash		16,000	8,000

The balance of the accounts receivable in the general balance is $8000 and this amount is equivalent to the summation of the individual ledgers mentioned in the subsidiary ledger. The balance of the control account mentioned in the general ledger will always be equal to the total of the balances mentioned in the concerned in which ledger accounts. If these balances are equal, then it shows an error in the books of accounts.

Here are the reasons why a business will use subsidiary journalists instead of maintaining just one general journal.

All transactions of a similar nature will be collected in one place. For instance, all the credit sales recorded in the sales book. This, in turn, helps to post any impersonal accounts along with the balances.

It also helps with the division of responsibilities. For instance, the posting of a certain ledger can be entrusted to different workers at the same time. Therefore, the accounts of a large company can be written up quickly. It also helps to introduce internal checks.

Whenever entries are recorded in the subsidiary journals, enables a business to record more details that cannot be included in a general ledger.

Whenever transactions of a similar nature are collected in one place, it enables the accountant to perform a careful survey of any trend, pattern of distribution, and other helpful. All this information in handy while making any day-to-day decisions about the operation of a business. For instance, a careful analysis of those sales return ledger can help understand the cause of such returns along with any loss sustained in this process.

Trial Balance

Trial balance is a report of bookkeeping or accounting that will list out the balances in all the general ledger accounts of an organization. There will be a column labeled as "debit balances" and the debit balance amounts are listed here. Another column labeled "credit balances" will have a list of all the credit balance accounts. When the total is calculated for each column, they should be the same.

Once all the accounts have been balanced off, they are placed in a list with credit balances on one side and debit balances on the other. This list is referred to as a trial balance. Since most of the accounting records are based on the double entry system, the trial balance needs to tally. If the totals on both sides current arithmetically correct, then must be some error in the preparation of the books of accounts. However, just because the balances tally doesn't mean that the trial balance is free of all errors. Here are the main characteristics of a trial balance.

- This statement is prepared in a tabular form. It consists of two columns, one for credit balances and the other foot debit balances.
- The balances obtained from a ledger account for the closing balances are shown in the trial balance.
- The trial balance is not a statement and account per se and is merely a statement of all balances.
- As long as the ledger accounts are balanced, trial balance can be prepared whenever required.
- It provides a consolidated list of the ledger balances at the end of a given period.

- Trial balance is used for checking the arithmetical accuracy of all the ledger accounts.
- Trial balance is used for creating other financial statements like profit and loss account, trading account, and the balance sheet as well.
- Here are the reasons why a trial balance is usually prepared.
- The first reason is that it has strictly arithmetical accuracy of the books of accounts.
- If there is any error while creating the subsidiary books or records, it will be immediately reflected in the trial balance.
- If there is any error in the posting of entries to the subsidiary books, even that can be easily figured out.
- A trial balance makes it easier to verify the schedules of debtors as well as creditors.
- Any error regarding balancing of accounts can also be checked using the trial balance.

Limitations of a trial balance

Keep in mind that a trial balance is never conclusive proof of accuracy of the books of accounts. Even if the trial balance tallies, it doesn't necessarily mean that the books of accounts are free of all errors. There are some errors that remain undetected or undisclosed while preparing a trial balance. This is perhaps the major limitation of this statement. In this section, let us look at certain errors that are disclosed by trial balance.

If an entry has been omitted from the original book of records, then it will not reflect on the trial balance. Since both the aspects of a transaction have been completely left off the books of accounts, it will never make it to the trial balance. According to the system of double entry, every transaction needs to have a credit as well as debit aspect to it. Because both of these aspects have never made it to the original book of records, this error will be left undetected. For instance, if goats were sold to ABC on credit, and this fact was never included in the sales journal, it will neither appear on the debit side of ABCs account not the credit side of the sales account.

If an item has been posted to the correct side bar to the wrong account, even then it will not appear in the trial balance for instance if cash was received from ABC but this transaction has been wrongly credited to XYZ instead of ABC's account, even if the amount is correct, there will be no imbalance in the trial balance.

Another error that is left undetected by trial balance is one wrong amount has been entered in the subsidiary books of accounts. For instance, a credit purchase of $4000 was wrongly entered in the purchases book as $400; the error will not show up in the trial balance.

All sorts of compensating errors will not be reflected in the trial balance. For instance, any amount of excess debit or under debit of an account can be neutralized if there is excess credit or under credit to the same quantum on other accounts. This isn't a usual occurrence, but if the amounts compensate for each other, it will never show up on the trial balance. For instance, if an accountant forgets to post $1000 to the debit side of a specific account and then under-posts $1000 to the credit side of another account, the trial balance will tally.

Any error caused due to a wrongly applied principle of accounting will not show up in the trial balance. Whenever a specific amount isn't properly allocated between revenue and capital or whenever a principle of double entry is violated, it is referred to as an error of principle. For instance, if salaries paid to employees are debited to the salaries account, it is an error of principle. Likewise, if the proprietor of a sole proprietorship with straws any goods for personal use, it needs to be debited to the Drawings account and simultaneously credited to the Purchases account.

Preparing a trial balance

A trial balance is not the same as a financial statement. It is more of an internal report that was helpful when manual accounting was done. An imbalance in the trial balance will indicate errors somewhere between the trial balance and journal. This error is usually because of some miscalculation in account balance, posting credit amounts as debit, etc. The accounting software used in the current day has eliminated the chances of such errors. This is why trial balance is not as important as it once was. Now the trial balance and general ledger will quite surely have balanced debits and credits. Auditors and accountants still find trial balance useful in some ways.

Trial balance will have the following information:

- Titles of every general ledger account with a balance
- Two columns on the right of the account titles that will be labeled as debit and credit.
- Every account balance will be listed in the appropriate columns.
- Summary of every column after all the account balances are entered.
- Equal total on the debit column and credit column.

CHAPTER FIVE

FINANCIAL STATEMENTS

What Is A Financial Statement?

Money is often invested in a business to earn profits. To a certain this, it is quintessential that an accountant needs to measure and accurate accounting data in a systematic manner so that the amount of profit on or the loss incurred by the business can be determined as well as reported. It is important to a certain the profits earned to calculate income tax, dividends, and for preparing any future plans of expansion. To determine the profit earned a loss incurred, a statement known as the income statement is prepared. All the items regarding expenses and losses along with revenues and gains occurring within an accounting period are included in the income statement. There is another statement that is prepared to understand the financial position of a business on the last date of the accounting period known as the balance sheet. All these statements together are known as financial statements. They're also referred to as the final accounts of a company because there often calculated at the end of the financial accounting process. The information in these statements comes from the balances appearing in the trial balance.

A financial statement is a systematic and written record related to the business activities along with the financial performance of the company. The income statement concentrates on the revenues and expenses of a company during a specific period. When the expenses are subtracted from the total revenue earned by a company, it produces a figure known as the net income. The balance sheet gives an overview of all the liabilities, assets, and stockholder's equity for a given timeframe. The cash flow statement helps to analyze whether the company has sufficient cash to meet its debt obligations, funding its investments, and managing its operating expenses.

Well, there are certain limitations applicable to the financial statements as well. They certainly provide a lot of information, but these statements are open to interpretation. The way an investor interprets this financial data can vary from one person to another. For instance, an investor might be looking to see whether a company has repurchased the stalks or not while another one might prefer to see that the company is investing money in long-term assets. One investor might be fine with the existing debt level of a company, whereas another in Best might be concerned about the company's debt levels.

Five financial statements should be included when a corporation distributed its annual statements. These are:

- Income statement
- Statement of comprehensive income

- Balance sheet
- Statement of stockholder's equity
- Cash flow statement

Notes to the financial statements also have to be included with these. The notes are used to disclose information about undisclosed amounts that are important but not in the financial statement.

When distributing financial statements, the company has to comply with the generally accepted accounting principles or GAAP rules. The majority of amounts in the financial statements will be from the records of past transactions. This is why these amounts may not always be relevant to future decision-making and cannot indicate what the current fair market value of the company is.

Where do the amounts come from?

The amounts that are reported in financial statements will generally originate from the companies recorded and stored business transactions in their general ledger books. It is to be noted that Accounting records are usually referred to as books.

Accountants record not only business transactions but also the adjusting entries. Adjusting entries are important for various reasons, including:

Certain recorded transaction amounts may pertain to more than a single accounting period. This accounting period could be weeks, months, years, etc. Adjusting entries are required so that pertinent amounts are all that is included in the financial statements of a particular period.

There may be expenses that occurred very late in the accounting period, and these could not be processed or recorded in the general ledger accounts. To include these expenses in the financial statements, accrual type adjusting entries will have to be recorded by the accountant.

GAAP also required other adjusting entries like adjustments for uncollectible accounts receivable or adjustments for some marketable securities if the fair market value is different.

Accounting periods

Corporations are compelled to issue their annual financial statements. However, it is also common for them to prepare these financial statements every month. The period can be anything from a month, three months, six months, a year, etc. A lot of companies have their accounting year beginning on 1st January and end on 31st December. However, others could have a financial year that begins on 1st July in one year and ending on 30th June of next year. Such financial years are called fiscal years. Certain companies have fiscal years based on weeks and not months as well. A fiscal year is beneficial because it will coincide with a business year.

Users of financial statements

Financial statements that are issued by a company will find their way to the following people or groups:

- Current lenders
- Current stockholders
- Potential future lenders
- Potential future investors
- Financial analysts
- Current as well as future goods and services suppliers
- Certain customers
- Labor unions
- Government agencies
- Competitors

Users tend to compare financial statements to previous accounting periods or other companies. This is why it is important that the common reporting rules are followed in the financial statements. You have learned about the requirements of GAAP in a previous section of the book.

Capital and Revenue Expenditure and Receipts

Final accounts are prepared at the end of the year and they consist of the income statement, balance sheet, cash flow statement, and the statement of retained earnings. All the accounts, which appear in the trial balance, are taken to either the income statement or the balance sheet. In order to decide which item goes where, the following principle of accounting is applied. All revenue expenditures along with receipts are taken to the income statement while all capital expenditure and capital receipts are entered in the balance sheet. It is, therefore, essential to realize the importance of distinction between capital and revenue items because any error in these items can lead to falsification of final accounts.

A capital expenditure is one that increases the value at which a fixed or a capital asset may properly be carried on in the books. All expenditure that results in the acquisition of any permanent assets that are intended to be continually used in the business purpose of earning revenue I'd deem to be capital expenditure. The term capital expenditure is usually used for signifying an expenditure, which increases the quantity of fixed assets, quality of fixed assets, or results in the replacement of fixed assets.

An amount that is spent by the business for earning or providing revenue is referred to as revenue expenditure. Revenue expenditure is one that constitutes a proper deduction from income revenue. It is an expense. In other words, all establishments and other expenses incurred in the conduct and administration of the business are deemed to be revenue expenditures. All expenses incurred by the way of repairs, replacement of existing assets, which not only add to their earning capacity but simply serve to maintain the original equipment in an efficient working condition are charged as revenue expenditures. Examples of revenue expenses include any expenditure incurred during the normal course of business. For instance, expenses of Administration, expenses incurred in manufacturing and selling products, expenses related to salaries, rent and repair of facets and so on. All those expenses which are incurred for maintaining the business like the replacement of any existing permanent assets, costs of stores consumed for manufacturing and so on are also deemed to be revenue expenditures.

Deferred revenue expenditure is the term that's used for describing any expenditure of a revenue nature with its benefits spread over a couple of years. Some common examples of deferred revenue income include preliminary expenses, brokerage payable on issue of shares, expenses incurred in shifting a business, or even any exceptional repairs. All these might look like expenses but when it comes to accounting, they aren't treated as regular expenses. Given the massive amounts involved, these expenses cannot be written off in a single financial year. If such expenses are written off from a single year's profits, then there might be no profits left. To prevent this and to maintain a profitable venture, deferred revenue expenses are written off from the income statement on a yearly basis. The unwritten portion of the deferred revenue expenditure will be reflected on the assets side of the balance sheet.

All capital receipts are reflected in the balance sheet and the revenue receipts in the income statements. Capital receipts include the proceeds from the sale of fixed assets, issue of any shares or debentures, and money received in the form of loans. Any funds obtained in the due course of business are known as revenue receipts. Revenue receipts include any proceeds from the sale of goods, interest received on deposits, or even dividend on any investments.

Income Statement

Income statements are financial statements that report the revenues, expenses, and net income of a company. The balance sheet of a company is concerned only with a particular point in time. However, the income statement will cover a period of a time interval.

Amongst other financial statements, the income statement is an important statement that accountants or business owners use. It is also referred to as a statement of income, statement of operators or profit and loss statement.

It is important because it will indicate the profitability of that company in a specific time interval that is mentioned in its heading. This period of time will be decided by the business and can vary for everyone. Remember that the income statement will show expenses, losses, gains, and revenues. It will not show cash disbursements or cash receipts.

The profitability of the company is given special attention due to various reasons. For instance, when a company cannot operate profitably, a bank or creditor will be unwilling to provide any more funds to the company. However, if the company is working profitably, it will be demonstrating its ability to use any borrowed money successfully. Lenders or investors need to see if the company has the ability to function profitably before they know they can invest more money in it. It is also of concern to others like competitors, labor unions, consonant management or government agencies.

Items included

The income statement format will vary depending on the complexity of the business activities of a company. However, the following elements will be included in the income statements for most companies:

Revenues and gains

Operating revenue

All the income that comes from primary activities of a business is referred to as operating revenue. For instance, if a company is involved in the manufacturing of a product, then the revenue from primary activities will be the income obtained from the sale of its products. For a wholesaler, the operating revenue will come from the sales of the products he offers. Likewise, for a company that offers services, the operating revenue will be generated from the fees or revenue earned in exchange for its services.

Net-operating revenue

Any income generated from the non-core or secondary activities of a business is known as non-operating income. This income originates from earnings that are generated from sources other than the sale and purchase of goods or services. It usually includes any income that business earns from its investments, rental income from business property, receipts of royalty payment, or any other income generated from advertising placed on the business's property.

Gains

Gains are also referred to as other income. This refers to the net income, which was made from other activities such as the sale of any long-term assets. It also includes any income that was realized from a one-time activity, which isn't related to the business like the sale of a subsidiary company, of unused land, or any other property owned by the business. Revenue and receipts are two different things. Any income, which is made from the sales of products or services provided will be termed as revenue for a specific period. Receipts refer to the cash that is received and will be accounted for only when the money is actually received. For instance, if a customer purchases goods on credit on 15th September and promises to repay by 15th October, then this transaction will be recorded only when the amount is actually received by the business.

Expenses and losses

The cost that business in cause to continue its operations and earn a profit is referred to as an expense. There are certain expenses that can be written off as a tax return if the IRS guidelines provide for it.

Primary activity expenses

All the expenses that a business incurs in its usual day-to-day operations, which are directly associated with the primary activity of the business are referred to as primary activity expenses. Primary activity expenses include selling costs, administrative expenses, depreciation, R&D expenses, cost of goods sold, and even amortization. The usual items included in this section include the wages payable to workers, salaries payable to employees, expenses toward utility bills, and sales commissions.

Secondary activity expenses

All the expenses incurred by a business that are directly related to its primary activities are referred to as secondary activity expenses. It usually includes expenses like any interest paid on loan. Losses are also treated as expenses. Any loss that is incurred from the sale of a long-term asset or any other unusual costs such as unexpected lawsuits will be treated as expenses.

The primary expenses and revenue of business provide insight into whether the company's core business is doing well or not. Whereas, the secondary expenses and revenue accounts show the company's expertise while managing its non-core activities. If the income from the sale of the goods produced by a company is lower than the income that it receives from interest on the bank account, it shows that accompanies and utilizing its funds properly. If the company is gaining any recurring income by hosting billboards at a factory, then it shows that the company is capitalizing on its resources and increasing its profitability. The income statement essentially shows whether the company's funds are being utilized optimally or not.

The formula used for calculating the Net Income is as follows.

Net Income = (Gains + Revenue) – (Expenses + Losses)

Let us look at an example to get a better understanding of the way that income is calculated. Let us assume that a fictitious company, ABC produces sports merchandise and offers sports training too. The company received a total of $25,000 from the sale of its goods in the first quarter. It also received an additional $5000 from the training services it offers. Its primary expenses amounted to $10,500. It also received $1000 from the sale of unused machinery and lost $800 from the settlement of a lawsuit. So, the net income of this company comes to $19700.

This is referred to as a single-step income statement. It is perhaps the simplest forms of income statement there is. However, seldom do companies in the real world have such straightforward income statements. Most companies have a rather diversified array of business segments and usually, get involved in mergers or acquisitions and also form any strategic partnerships. Given the complexities of a modern-day company, they usually follow a multi-step income statement. In this method, all the different items listed in an income statement are segregated.

The net amount should be positive when the expenses and losses are subtracted from revenues and gains. This will be labeled as net income. It will be a net loss if the net amount comes out to be negative.

Amounts on Income statements

The amounts that are shown on the company's income statement will reflect many transactions that the accounting system recorded. Adjusting entry amounts will also be entered to comply with the accrual accounting method.

Revenues are what the company earns from its main activities. This will include selling products that are reported as net product revenue, net sales, etc. It will also include providing services that are reported as revenues or net service revenues. Revenues will be reported in the income statement in that period in which they are earned. These are captured when the sales invoices are usually prepared. Accountants prepare adjusting entries at the end of that accounting period and include any revenue that might not have been processed by the accounting system as well.

Expenses are historical costs associated with the main business activities of a company and reported on their income statement. Costs end up as expenses in income statements in four ways. One is when they beat match revenues. The second is when they were used or expired. The third is when no future value is there that can be measured. The fourth is when the cost is too small for justifying allocation to a future period.

Gains and losses are recorded on disposals of assets. The received amount should not be included in revenues when an asset is it longer used by a company.

Balance Sheet

Balance sheets are statements of financial position. They reflect the accounting equation of a company or sole proprietor. These balance sheets will report the assets, liabilities, and stockholder's equity of a company at a specific point. The balance sheet is the accounting equation and will display that the company has total assets equal to the sum of its liabilities and stockholder's equity.

Accounting balance sheets are major financial statements that accountants or business owners use.

Since the balance sheet will be representing the financial position of the company at a specific date, it is often considered a financial snapshot in time. The balance sheet will inform any reader of the financial position of the company at some point in time. This allows people like creditors to check what the company's assets and liabilities are at that point. This kind of information is valuable for bankers who need to determine whether they should approve loans or credit for a company. Current investors, suppliers, company management, labor unions, etc. are also invested in this information from the balance sheet.

The balance sheet is prepared with the primary aim to understand the desires financial position of a business on the last date of its financial year. Different balances of nominal accounts like salaries, wages, rent and commission, and so on from the trial balance transferred to the trading on the profit and loss account. Various real accounts, as well as personal accounts related to the customers, are placed under the heading- sundry debtors. Similarly, all balances due to the suppliers are grouped under the heading- sundry creditors. All real and personal account balances are grouped into two categories of assets and liabilities.

The balance sheet is a precise statement of financial position. It will be prepared only after the completion of the trading on the profit and loss account. All the items that were not included in the trading in the profit and loss account will be divided into assets and liabilities, which will find a place in the balance sheet. Liabilities to present the credit balances on the ledger, whereas the assets represent the debit balances. The balance sheet is always prepared at a specific date and shows the business's financial position on that date.

There are three important terms that are used in the balance sheet, and they are assets, equity, and liabilities. In this section, let us look at a couple of important terms that are used in the balance sheet.

As mentioned in the previous chapters, assets represent any tangible objects along with the intangible value that a business owns. Assets can be classified as fixed assets and current assets. A current asset is a term which is used to describe cash in other assets along with resources commonly believed as those which can be readily sold or consumed during the normal operating cycle of a business. The normal operating cycle of businesses about 12 months, but at times it can be longer than that. So, different prepayment of expenses like prepaid insurance, salary paid in advance, or even rent paid in advance will be classified as current assets. Other current assets include cash balance, bank balance, temporary investment, debtors, stock in trade, any payments made in advance, and all bills receivables. Any asset that provides any service or helps to increase the value of a business and is held for a longer period is defined as fixed assets. Fixed assets include tangible assets like land, equipment, plant and building, furniture and fixtures, machinery and such. It also includes intangible assets such as patents, trademarks, and goodwill.

Equity represents anything that has been enforced against the assets of a business. Claims can be made against the assets of a business by owners as well as creditors, and they are both termed as equities. So, equity refers to a claim that the following have:

- Creditors of a business,
- Owners of a business,
- Creditors as well as owners of a business.

So, Equity = Assets

Or, Liabilities + Shareholder's Equities = Assets.

Any claim that has been made against the assets of a business by the creditors is referred to as liabilities. Liabilities can include long-term liabilities of fixed liabilities and current liabilities. Please refer to the information given in "Chapter 1" to learn more about liabilities.

Cash Flow Statement

Cash flow statements are officially known as the statement of cash flows. It is one of the main financial statements of a corporation. This cash flow statement will report the cash that is generated and used in a time interval that is specified in the heading of the statement. The company can decide what this period is.

The statement of cash flow will organize and report what cash was generated or used under the following categories:

- Operating activities. Items reported on an income statement from the accrual method of accounting are converted to cash.
- Investing activities. The purchase or sale of any long-term investments, properties, plants, and equipment are reported.
- Financing activities. Insurance or repurchase of the company's bonds, stock, and dividend payments are recorded.
- Supplemental information. Exchange of any significant items not involving cash is reported. The interest and income tax amount paid is also reported.

So, what does the statement of cash flow tell you?

Income statements are prepared with the help of accrual basis of accounting. Due to this, there is a change that the revenues were not collected. The expenses that were reported on that income statement might also not have been paid. The balance sheet changes can be reviewed to determine what the facts are. However, the cash flow statement will have integrated this information already. This is why cash flow statements are utilized by savvy businesspeople or investors.

Points to note are:

- Other than cash, if an asset increases, there will be a decrease in the cash account.
- Other than cash, if an asset decreases, there will be an increase in the cash account.
- There will be an increase in cash account if liability increases.
- There will be a decrease in the cash account if liability decreases.
- There will be an increase in cash account if there is an increase in owner's equity.
- There will be a decrease in cash account if there is a decrease in owner's equity.

Cash flow statement format

There are four distinct sections in a cash flow statement:

- Cash involving operating activities
- Cash involving investing activities
- Cash involving financing activities

- Supplemental information

If the indirect method is used to prepare the statement of cash flow, important information can be acquired from the differences in the balance sheet accounts of a company.

Cash involving operating activities:

This section will report the net income of the company and also convert it to cash basis from the accrual basis with the changes in the balances of current liability and current asset accounts like:

- Accounts receivable
- Supplies
- Inventory
- Prepaid insurance
- Notes payable
- Accounts payable
- Wages payable
- Payroll taxes payable
- Unearned revenues
- Interest payable
- Other current assets
- Other current liabilities

This section will also have adjustments for depreciation expenses, losses, and gains from long-term asset sales.

Cash involving investing activities

This section will report the changes in the long-term asset account balances like:

- Land
- Equipment
- Long term investment
- Vehicles
- Furniture

It involves the sale or purchase of any long-term investment, plant, property, and equipment.

Cash involving financing activities

This section will report the balance changes of longer-term liabilities and stockholder's equity accounts like:

- Bonds payable
- Preferred stock
- Notes payable
- Common stock
- Deferred income taxes
- Treasury stock

Retained earnings

These financial activities will involve repurchase or issuance of the company's bonds or stocks and also borrowings or repayments that are long term and short term.

Supplemental information

This section in the statement will disclose the interest amount and paid income taxes. Significant exchanges that did not involve cash will also be reported.

Certain adjustments are made to the net income of a company by adding or subtracting any differences in revenue, credit transactions, and expenses. These adjustments help calculate the cash flow of a business. All non-cash items are included in the income statement, whereas all assets and liabilities are included in the balance sheet. The cash flow statement helps fill up the gap between these two statements by making a place for all the adjustments made by a business. There are two methods that can be used for preparing the cash flow statement, and they are the direct method and the indirect method.

Direct method

The direct method is quite straightforward. It essentially is a summation of the different types of cash payments as well as the receipts of a company. It includes the cash paid to suppliers, cash received from customers, and any cash paid out as salaries. All these figures are calculated by using the opening and closing balances of different types of business accounts. It helps to examine any net increase or decrease in business accounts.

Indirect method

The cash flow from operating activities in the indirect method is calculated by using the net income of a company from its income statement. Since the income statement of a company is prepared on the accrual basis, revenue will only be recognized when it is turned and not when received. The net income is not an accurate representation of the cash flow from operating activities. There are certain items that affect the net income, and it becomes quintessential to adjust any earnings before interest and taxes. This needs to be done even if no cash has been paid or received against them. The indirect method also makes provisions for adding back any non-operating activities that don't affect the operating cash flow of a company. For instance, depreciation is not a cash expense. Depreciation is the amount that is deducted from the value of an asset. Since it is not a cash expense, it must be added to the net sales to calculate the cash flow for the company. Only when an asset is sold will the income from might be included in a cash flow statement.

Accounts receivable

There will be certain changes in the accounts receivable present on a balance sheet from an accounting period to the other. This change needs to be represented in the cash flow statement. If the amount of accounts receivable decreases, it shows that more cash has entered the organization. This is usually in the form of cash received because customers are paying off their credit accounts. The amount by which the accounts receivable has decreased will be added to the net sales. If the accounts receivable has increased from one period to the next, then the increase needs to be deducted from the net sales.

Inventory value

If a company purchases raw material and spends more of its funds doing this, then there will be an increase in the inventory. If the inventory was acquired using cash, then any increase in the value of the inventory will be deducted from the net sales of the company. Likewise, any decrease in the inventory will be added to the net sales. There will be an increase in accounts payable if the inventory was purchased on credit, and the same will be reflected on the balance sheet. The amount of increase from one year to the other in inventory levels will be added to the net sales. The same criteria are used for taxes payable, prepaid insurance, and any salaries payable. If an expense has been paid off, then the difference between the value owed from one year and the next must be subtracted from the net income. If there is an outstanding amount, then any differences need to be added to the net earnings.

Investing activities

Any sources of cash, along with its use from a company's investments, are referred to as investing activities. For instance, purchase or sale of an asset, payments received from customers or loans made to a vendor, or any payments related to a merger and acquisition will be included in this category. Essentially, investing activities relates to any changes in assets, investments, or equipment related to cash generated from investing. Any changes from investing activities are referred to as cash out items since cash needs to be spent on acquiring new equipment or other short-term assets. However, whenever a company sells or divests its assets, the transaction is a cash-in since cash is entering the business.

Financing activities

The cash that is used for and incurred from financing activities is included in the section. It includes the source of cash from investors or banks and also the cash, which was used for paying any shareholders. So, the payment of dividends, payment made to repurchase talk, and along with the repayment of debt will be included in this category. Whenever capitalists raised, there will be cash from financing activities. Likewise, when a dividend is paid, it is a cash-out transaction. So, if a company issues its shares to the public, the company will receive financing. However, whenever it pays dividends to its shareholders, the company's cash reserves will reduce.

Positive cash flow is always a sign of a healthy business. It isn't necessary that a cash flow statement needs always to represent a positive cash flow. It doesn't mean that negative cash flow is a red flag. At times, negative cash flow can be because a company is expanding its business. By analyzing any changes in the cash flow from one period to the next will enable an investor to understand whether a company is performing well or not.

Balance sheet and income statement

A cash flow statement is prepared using the information collected from the income statement and the balance sheet. The net earnings calculated from the income statement is the balance from which all the other information included in the cash flow statement is deducted. Any net cash flow in the cash flow statement from one year to the next needs to be equal to the increase or decrease of cash reserves between the two consecutive balance sheets is applicable to the period within which the cash flow statement is created. For instance, if the cash flow is calculated for the year 2018, then the balance sheet from the year 2017 and 2018 need to be used.

A cash flow statement is a valuable tool, which helps to measure the profitability and the strength of a company. It helps determine whether a company has sufficient funds for meeting its expenses or not. It also helps to predict the future cash flow of the business. It is often used while budgeting. The cash flow statement provides investors with a bird's eye view of the company's financial health. The greater the cash available, the better is it for the company. It also helps the investor understand whether the company is optimally using its funds or not.

Statement of Retained Earnings

Retained earnings are the cumulative amount of earnings from the time a corporation was formed minus the amount of the cumulative dividend that it has declared since then. Simply put, retained earnings are the past earnings of the corporation that have not been distributed to stockholders of the corporation. The retained earnings of a corporation are reported separately in stockholders' equity section of a balance sheet. Even when there is a significantly large amount of positive retained earnings in a corporation, it cannot be assumed that they subsequently have a lot of cash. Corporations tend to use their cash to buy a new property, plant, or equipment. They might also use it to reduce the liabilities of the company. When the retained earnings of the corporation are a negative amount, the term "deficit" will be used and not retained earnings.

Statement of retained earnings is a statement that will show the changes from one point to another in retained earnings.

The retained earnings of a corporation are not distributed to their stockholders as dividends because the money is used for strengthening the financial position of the company. It is also used of expansion of operations or for keeping up with inflation even while trying to maintain the current operations. The corporation requires the money for various purposes. Stockholders may ask to prefer to have the money used for such purposes because it will help increase the value of the company's stock. This is why they prefer foregoing dividends and instead want better use madc of retained earnings. For individuals who are in the higher income tax brackets, getting dividends would mean that 40% of their money goes towards taxes. However, if they forego the dividend, their stock value will increase, and no tax payments are involved. When they sell their stock, they will just have to pay a much lower tax towards capital gains.

The equation used for computing the retained earnings of a company is as follows.

Retained earnings at the end = Retained earnings at the beginning + Net income – Dividends.

CHAPTER SIX

MANAGERIAL ACCOUNTING

Managerial accounting is also known as management accounting or cost accounting. It is the process that involves identification, measurement, analysis, interpretation as well as communication of information to managers to attain the goals of their company. The main difference network financial accounting and managerial accounting is that the latter is aimed at helping managers within the organization to make decisions while the former is aimed at helping people outside the organization.

Managerial accounting will include any part of accounting that is aimed at providing business operations metrics to management. The information that is related to product cost or services is used by managerial accountants. Budgets are also used for the plan of operation of a business in a quantitative way of expression. Managerial accountants will utilize all performance reports to check for any deviation in the actual results from the given budget.

Marginal Analysis

Determination of the incremental change in profit or other gain associated with many possible alternatives is done using Marginal Analysis. The decision of choosing the alternative depends on the outcome of the analysis. A wise man must always choose the alternative that provides the maximum incremental profit. The above concept is used to maximize an organization's gains. The marginal analysis concepts are followed in many aspects, and some of them are:

- Manufacturer decision: if additional units should be sold at a reduced price to a customer.
- Personal decision: if you should do overtime or take a vacation
- Government decision: if the government should fund a public program to offer better or extra services to taxpayers.

For instance, an ice-cream parlor owner gets an order from a customer for 100 choc-bars at a price of $20 each. The ice-cream parlor owner calculates and estimates a good profit on 80 units. After that the remaining 20 units, he will have to pay his staff overtime, which doesn't make any profit from the remaining 20 units. So marginal analysis concept tells him to take an order of 80 units and make extra 20 units only if the customer pays extra money for the remaining 20 units.

Another example – suppose a phone manufacturing company is working very hard and producing the maximum number of phones up to their capacity. Still, there is more demand for these phones on the market. So, the management will be hesitant to invest in opening an additional production center. Instead, they invest in expanding the current production facility in small increments and check if the profit margin is still maintained, so this is a marginal analysis where the management is careful and taking better decisions in expanding than to build another reproduction facility and not know if the profit can be achieved accordingly.

Contribution margin analysis

Contribution margin analysis produces the residual margin after variable expenditures are subtracted from the total revenue. The amount of money spent on various products and services can be differentiated using contribution margin analysis, from which the management can then decide which products are doing better and which of them should be focused more by increasing the ad campaign and better marketing plans. Management can compare the contribution made and the total amount of fixed costs to be given in each period of time so that the management comes to an end if the current pricing and the cost value of the business is going to make profits or not

Contribution margin is calculated by subtraction all variable expenses from the revenue. The percentage contribution margin is generated by dividing the outcome with the revenue. Overhead cost is not mentioned in this calculation.

Contribution margin analysis is also used to determine the contributions of achievement targets under the process, to check if anyone would pay enough cash for a product or a service. And if it's not worth, the in-charge must then decide if the price should be reduced so that therein profit and sale increases also.

The disadvantage of this type of analysis is that it doesn't consider the impact of products and services on the company's constraint; it's the main component for a company's high-profit achievement. When a high contribution margin product takes a longer time than the usual time, the end result would be less profit all in all because the other products are made in the remaining time and very limited time is left at the constraint. The above-mentioned conflict can be resolved by increasing the contribution margin analysis to envelope the consumption of the contribution per minute in the given time. Companies should focus on the products and services with the highest margin per minute, as they should be selling faster.

Some of the aspects are not given proper attention, and one of them is the price points included in the calculation of the contribution margin analysis. It can, in fact, be of great significance based on its use of volume discounts, special promotions, which will eventually lead to high revenue portion, which can lead to high expected contribution margins.

Constraint Analysis

Constraint analysis concentrates on the bottlenecks in an organization. So, the manager of a company should be concentrating only on the maximum usage of a bottleneck as the bottleneck helps to increase the profits of the business. Other than the bottleneck, other aspects will bring no change in profit. It's a very important concept as bottleneck can be found in any part of the business. For example, if a production company requires a high degree of technical knowledge and all the staff members of the company are fully occupied, then the sales or profit is not going to increase unless the company hires new staff members. And another example is if a production company produces 100 units of candies unless they don't buy a new machine, the current one cannot produce more than 100 as it produces to its maximum capacity.

The theory of constraints

The theory of constraints states any organization, or any system has a choke point, and the choke point prevents it from achieving its goals. The choke point, which is also called as bottleneck or constraint, must be managed carefully for the smooth operation of the business at any given time. Or else, it will be difficult to achieve the goals. The cause of the above-mentioned line is because unless the capacity of the contract is not increased, there will be no extra throughput (subtract all variable expenses from revenue).

The theory of constraints goes against the usual orthodox method of doing business, in which all the operations are performed at their maximum capacity level. From constraints point of view, maximizing all the performances of the business means it will increase the inventory, which will pile up, without any increase in profit. Therefore, proving that increasing the operations will only lead to an increase in inventory and not in profit.

Example of a constrained operation

A sofa production company finds out that their bottleneck is sponge production. Sponge production can produce only 30 sponges in a day and not more than that. So, if the company makes more than 30 sofa parts, then the remaining parts after 25 units should be kept in the storeroom. And it will only keep peeling and increase the cost of working capital.

So, the manager then finds out that it is wisest to return to only 30 units - production of all parts along with the sponge - so that the production and profit consistency remains stable.

Inventory buffers

It is extremely important to maximize the capacity in a constrained operation every time. One of the best ways to do it is by building an inventory buffer in front of the constraint operation. This inventory buffer will assure that any shortage of production of any parts of the operation will not hamper the continuous process or production of the product and it usually fluctuates in size as it gets used and replenished.

The performance of a company can improve by installing a sprint capacity in the production areas of the company.

Sprint Capacity

Sprint capacity is an increasingly high amount of production capacity that is assembled in the factories or workstations. When a mishap happens in the factory, and it cannot be avoided, the continuous flow of parts is stopped, and that's when sprint capacity is required. In this phase, the bottleneck takes resources from inventory buffer, which ends up in shortage in inventory buffer. So extra sprint capacity is required to mass-produce parts to refill the parts shortage in inventory buffer so that it can be used in the next unavoidable mishap.

It's a wise decision to invest in a large sprint capacity in a production company as it can rebuild the inventory buffer is a short span of time. So, if you can invest in a large sprint capacity, only a small investment is required for investment buffer. Or else if you invest in large inventory buffer, there will be less sprint capacity.

One of the main points we can learn here is that it is always a better option to maintain some space in the capacity in work areas and not limit the production capacity to the current needs.

Capital Budgeting

It is almost every company's motive and aims to expand their company in the future, and it is only possible if the company has good capital or good assets. And this capital, budgeting plays an important part in this process.

Every company uses a formal procedure to evaluate any potential investments or expenditures of significant value. This process is known as capital budgeting. It usually involves different decisions related to investing any existing funds for addition, modification, replacement, or even disposition of any fixed assets. Every company keeps making large expenditures from time to time. A couple of instances of large expenditures include the purchase of any fixed assets, acquiring new equipment, research and development projects, and so on. Each of these types of projects requires a rather large sum to be spent, and they are known as capital expenditures. Capital budgeting enables a company to maximize its future profits because a company can manage only a small number of massive projects at any given time.

Capital budgeting usually involves the following.

- The calculation of any future profit which can be generated by a project within a given period,
- The cash flow for a future period,
- The present value of the cash flow, along with the time value of money,

- The time is taken by the project to realize the initial investment,
- Risk analysis of the project and other factors.

Capital refers to the total investment made in a company, and budgeting is all about creating budgets and plans.

Some of the examples of capital expenditures are:

- Buying new equipment
- Repairing old equipment
- Buying delivery vehicles
- Constructing additions to old buildings

Few examples of Capital Budgeting Calculations

Capital budgeting includes the following calculations for every single project:

- Future accounting profit by period
- Future cash flows by period
- The present value of the cash flows by reducing them with an appropriate interest rate
- The time period is taken for a project's cash flow to return the initial cash investment
- An assessment of risk with the need to complete a project

Forecasting in Accounting

The process of utilizing the current and older cost data to predict future cost is called forecasting in accounting. It is important for organization purposes - it is important for a company to do estimation and organize money incurred before the actually incurring begins. These are the following methods used to forecast cost accounting:

- High-low method cost estimation
- Budgeting
- Regression analysis

Budgeting

Budgeting is the process of preparing a budget in order to plan for revenues and expenditures in an upcoming fiscal duration.

There are four objectives of budgeting, and these are the following:

- Facilitate the coordination and communication of these plans across the organization.
- Allocation of the resources within an organization.
- Managing the financial and operational performance of the members during the fiscal period.
- Evaluation of performances and producing goal-based incentives.

Budgets are made using current and historical data and estimations about upcoming trends. Traditional methods or zero-based methods can be used to prepare budgets. In the traditional method, they track the previous period's budgets and use it at the beginning of the upcoming period's budget whereas in the zero-based budget method they don't use any older records and start from scratch in each period.

High-low method

A method of estimating the forecasting is called high low method. It's a very simple method of estimating forecasting, but the accuracy is less than the more sophisticated methods like regression analysis.

In this technique, a set of data is required, which relates the cost-to-cost driver activities.

So, you have to consider the maximum cost and maximum cost driver activity and the minimum cost and minimum cost driver activity from the data set. Then you have to take out these four parts of the data to calculate the slope of the line, which connects two points. At last, you figure out the intercept using the slope and one of the points. And the end result will be the high, low-cost equation for that exact cost incurring activity.

Regression Analysis

A method of relating a dependent variable to an independent variable is known as regression analysis. This technique mainly functions to find out the value of the variance in the dependent variable due to variations in the independent variable. A set of data from both the dependent variable and the independent variable is required in regression analysis. The best platform for this analysis is in a computer program.

Regression analysis is of two types, and that is simple and multiple. In simple regression analysis, only one dependent variable and the independent variable is used. In multiple regression analysis, several independent variables are used, and only one dependent variable. The final outcome is it is an equation, which is used to predict costs depending on specific estimates of independent adjustable activity.

Cost Accounting

As the name suggests, cost accounting is that branch accounting which deals with companies cost of production. It does this by considering the input cost of every step of production along with fixed costs like depreciation of any fixed capital or capital equipment. All these costs are first individually recorded and measured. Once this is done, then the input results are compared with the output of all the actual results. Cost accounting enables management to measure the financial performance of a company. Cost accounting is used for decision-making. Financial accounting is the data, which is available to the investors. Financial accounting is the representation of different costs and financial performance, which includes the liabilities as well as the assets of a company. Cost accounting is one of the most beneficial tools for management while setting up any cost control programs and budgets to improve the net margins of the organization in the future. The main difference between financial accounting and cost accounting is that in financial accounting the costs are classified based on the type of transactions, whereas in cost accounting, the costs are classified based on the information required by the management. Unlike financial accounting, cost accounting doesn't have to follow any predefined rules or principles. Since it is a tool for internal management, it doesn't have to abide by the GAAP.

A lot of people tend to believe that cost accounting came about during the time of the industrial revolution. The growing economy of the industrial forces of demand and supply forced manufacturers to track the levels of there's talk along with the price of the same. Somewhere around the early 19th century, when David Ricardo was developing economic theories, famous writers like Charles Babbage were writing guides about how a business can manage its internal cost accounting. Cost accounting became an integral part of business management by the beginning of the 20th century.

Types of cost accounting

There are various types of cost accounting, and they are as follows.

Standard cost accounting

This form of cost accounting is based on ratios that are used to compare optimal use of labor along with material for producing goods or services under given conditions. Accessing and analyzing these differences is known as variance analysis. Traditionally, cost accounting essentially allocates costs based on a unit measure like labor or machine hours. Since the beginning of standard cost accounting, there has been a proportional increase in overhead costs and labor costs. Therefore, if the overhead cost is allocated as the overall cost, it doesn't always produce accurate insights. One of the major problems associated cost accounting is that this kind of accounting places more emphasis on labor efficiency than anything else. These days, labor efficiency makes for only a relatively small cost for most of the modern companies.

Activity-based costing

According to this form of cost, the overheads from every department are taken, and they are assigned to specific cost objects like customers, products, or services. An activity analysis is first performed to determine the way in which these costs must be assigned to their associated cost objects. During an activity analysis, the appropriate output measure is the essential cost driver. Activity-based costing is more accurate than standard cost accounting. Activity-based costing enables the management to understand the cost along with the profitability of the specific services or products offered by a company. Usually, this is conducted by passing out a survey to the employees of an organization who will then account for the time that they spend on different tasks. This gives the management a clear idea about the tasks that are time-consuming and the past in which most of the funds are spent.

Marginal costing

It is believed to be a simpler version of cost accounting. In marginal costing, the relationship that exists between the sales price of a product or service and the quantum of sales, the number of products produced, expenses incurred, costs, and the profits. This relationship is referred to as contribution margin. The contribution margin is usually obtained by dividing the revenue after subtracting any variable costs by the total revenue. This analysis is often used to understand the impact of changing cost on any potential profits. All the different factors that can influence the potential profit earning ability of the company can be analyzed by using marginal costing.

Types of costs

There are different types of costs, and they are fixed costs, variable costs, direct costs, and operating costs. Any cost that doesn't change according to the amount of work accompanied as is referred to as a fixed cost. The fixed cost usually includes items like the payment of rent on a building or a piece of equipment that they appreciate at a fixed value every month. Also, costs that change according to the company's level of production are referred to as variable cost.

The amount spent on making a product is known as product cost. The product cost includes direct materials, direct labor, consumable production supplies, and factory overhead. It can also be said that product cost is the cost of the labor needed to perform a service to a customer. In advanced cases, product cost also includes the total cost of a service provided like compensation, payroll taxes, and employee benefits. All those costs that are related to the day-to-day operations of the business are known as operating costs. These costs can be either a variable or fixed according to the given situation.

All the costs that are directly related to the production of a product are direct costs. For instance, if a coffee roaster spends about six hours roasting coffee beans, then the direct costs will include the cost of the coffee beans along with the cost of the labor.

Product cost

The product cost on a unit basis is derived by adding the total amount spent on direct labor, direct materials, consumable supplies, allocated overhead and the sum are divided by the total number of units.

The formula for calculating the product cost is as follows:

(Total direct labor + Total direct materials + Consumable supplies + Total allocated overhead) ÷ Total number of units = Product unit cost

This cost can be considered as an inventory asset of a company if the product is not sold. As soon as the product sells, the amount can be charged on the cost of the products sold. Then it will be mentioned as an expense on the revenue statement.

Product cost is mentioned in the financial statement of a company as it includes the production overhead that is required by GAAP and IFRS both. Managers can alter the product cost to cut the overhead component when they make short-term production and sale price decision. Some of the managers can also choose to concentrate more on the effect of a product on a bottleneck operation, which clearly indicates that they are focusing mainly on the total direct material cost of a product and the total time spent on bottleneck operation.

MRC
-TAX
M-
M+
+TAX

CONCLUSION

As we come to the end of the book, I would like to thank you again. I hope the book was helpful and you now have a much better understanding of accounting than you did before. You can see that a lot more is involved in accounting than the layman usually thinks. However, it is not really as complicated as some may think either. Understanding the basic concepts play a large role in it. Using the information given in this book, you can soon be on your way to becoming a great accountant. All the information in this book has been gathered from renowned and trustworthy sources. I hope it has helped you gain enough knowledge on financial and managerial accounting. Most of your questions on this subject will be answered if you read through the book thoroughly. Nonetheless, there is a lot of material available on accounting and you can always learn more.

If you found this book helpful, you may even recommend it to anyone else who needs a little help on the subject of accounting.

Thank you again and I wish you luck!

QUICKBOOKS

Step-by-Step Guide to Bookkeeping & Accounting for Beginners

By Kevin Ellis

outlined in this book.

By reading this document, the reader agrees that under no circumstances is the author responsible for any losses, direct or indirect, which are incurred as a result of the use of information contained within this document, including, but not limited to, — errors, omissions, or inaccuracies.

INTRODUCTION

Isn't it odd how your money always seems to disappear quicker than you earned it? You work hard day in and day out, and yet it never feels like you have enough. Worse, you constantly have to keep checking what you have because you don't remember. Did I have $200 left or only $150? Best login to the online banking to check. Oh, it's only $50.

If you have ever lived this experience, I don't need to tell you how awful it feels or how scary it is to experience it when running a business. What I do have to tell you is that you don't have to live this way. It is absolutely possible, even easy, to begin keeping track of your business's money. One of my all-time favorite tools for this is QuickBooks, and throughout this book, I will show you why.

QuickBooks is a bookkeeping and accounting software that you can download to use on your desktop or even just through the website at quickbooks.com. QuickBooks is designed to help you run your own business, keep track of inventory and income, and ultimately give you the tools to run your business easier. Not only that, but QuickBooks can also help you to take control of your personal finances as well, though this isn't its primary function. It is a truly versatile platform for all your accounting needs, and I know without a doubt that it can help you like it has helped me.

However, if you are new to accounting and bookkeeping, QuickBooks can seem a little intimidating. There's a ton of numbers and charts, and if you don't know what you're doing, then it can seem a little scary. That's why I've written this book. It is my goal to make getting started with QuickBooks as easy as possible so you can quickly learn the skills you need and begin bookkeeping like a pro.

To make sure that QuickBooks is right for you, we'll take a look at the advantages and disadvantages of the software. While I am fond of QuickBooks, not everyone is and your needs may be completely different than mine. By looking at the pros and cons, as well as the importance of an accounting system and the audience that QuickBooks markets to, you will be able to tell if it is the right fit for you.

In chapter two we look at the software itself. We'll take a look at the difference between the downloadable desktop version of Quickbooks and the version found online. It's surprising how much these two differ from price to third-party developer app integration. We'll cover all this plus look at the different types of plans that QuickBooks offers to see which are the best fit for your business.

Chapter three will cover everything you need to know to get started using QuickBooks. We'll take a look at the requirements necessary to begin using the software and will take an in-depth look at how to navigate around the QuickBooks interface. If you feel lost when you open up QuickBooks, this chapter will be your map through all the different sections. This chapter will even walk you through how to set up your first account, create your first customers, and input the vendors you work with.

Once you have accounts and customers in place, chapter four will dive deep into bookkeeping with QuickBooks. This chapter is packed full of useful guides on everything from creating your first invoice to paying your employees. We'll look at involves, credit memos, payroll, integrating bank accounts, and even keeping track of any inventory you have. By the end of the chapter, you will have the knowledge needed to do all your bookkeeping through QuickBooks.

We'll move from bookkeeping to accounting with chapter five. You'll be surprised to learn how easy it is to prepare financial statements using QuickBooks and start reporting. QuickBooks gives you tools to simplify the process so that it is downright simple when compared to working by hand and calculator. We'll also take a look at budgeting with QuickBooks in this chapter.

To close out, chapter six will be jam-packed with useful tips to help make getting started with QuickBooks as smooth as possible. Along with looking at how to outsource this work to an accountant or bookkeeper, this chapter will also get into how you keep your data safe. Your financial data is obviously not something you want to be stolen, so it is important that we follow safety protocols and procedures. This means that we avoid nasty mistakes that put our data at risk. We'll close with a look at some of these mistakes plus the less dangerous (but still annoying) ones that beginners often make.

By the end, you will have all the tools you need to use QuickBooks for your bookkeeping and accounting needs and really take control of your finances through the tools they offer.

CHAPTER ONE

WHY CHOOSE QUICKBOOKS

QuickBooks is a wonderful software, but it isn't perfect. It is a tool that we can use to handle our bookkeeping and accounting for our business. Just like a single screwdriver doesn't fit every screw, QuickBooks doesn't fit every business. If you bought this book, then I will assume you are a beginner to bookkeeping and accounting. If this notion is right, then there is a really good chance that QuickBooks will be the perfect tool for getting started.

But the first question that needs to be answered is: Why you would even want to use QuickBooks in the first place? What benefit is there to bookkeeping or accounting? By understanding why an accounting system is so valuable, you will be able to better understand why QuickBooks is such a useful tool.

Why is Having an Accounting System Important?

Accounting is simply the process of keeping financial accounts, while bookkeeping is focused on keeping records on financial information. When we talk, we typically lump bookkeeping in with accounting. When we say an accounting system, we are referring not just to a system of keeping financial accounts but a system for keeping accounts as well as the records of them. So an accounting system is really an accounting and bookkeeping system.

While a small business can get by with minimal bookkeeping, it is rare that any kind of successful business would willingly ignore such an important part of the process. As you work to build and grow your business, keeping track of all the financial data becomes a must. If you are the only employee and take care of all the purchasing and selling, then those numbers can do fine just in your head. While I wouldn't suggest keeping numbers this way, many starting businesses do just that.

But as the company begins to grow, an accounting system becomes a must. As employees are added, money is now heading out in different directions. Rather than just purchasing some inventory from a manufacturer, for example, you now have to purchase that inventory plus pay your employees. The more inventory you dabble in, the more divided your money becomes. The more employees, the more divided your money becomes. A good rule of thumb is that the more you grow, the more demands you will have on your money and the greater your need for a good accounting system will be.

While there are many different options available for accounting systems, we will be focusing on QuickBooks. However, the benefits of having an accounting system aren't determined by the system in use. Many systems, like QuickBooks, have pros and cons, but there are some very clear benefits to adopting an accounting system in general.

The first benefit of having an accounting system is that it gives you the data necessary to properly evaluate your business. Are you earning money or losing money? A good accounting system will keep records so that you have access to data about how your finances are doing today and how they were doing last month. By comparing the records, you can tell if your business is growing or if it is sinking. These records help you to evaluate how well your business is doing by making it easy to see if things are working or not compared to past practices.

Financial reports are a great way to tell where you are compared to where you have been, but one of the key features of an accounting system is that it gives you the tools to better manage your cash flow. The bigger the business is, the more directions cash will want to flow. The goal is to have more cash flow into the business than cash that flows out to pay for expenses. By understanding all the different directions that money is flowing, your accounting system will help you to see which areas you need to invest more money. From storefront renting costs to the price of the power or internet bills, there are a ton of different costs that a good accounting system will let you see and prepare for.

What happens if you know you want to grow your business but you aren't ready to just yet? You can track the company's growth using the financial records that you've made through your accounting system. By seeing how much growth your company has been undergoing, you can make predictions about future growth. A good accounting system helps you to get this information so that you can use it to set goals for where you want to be knowing that you have all the data you need to make a plan to get there. This means that an accounting system isn't just good for seeing where you have been or where the money is going in the present. An accounting system is also a valuable tool for seeing where your company is heading.

Is QuickBooks a Good Fit for You?

Chances are the answer is yes. If you are a beginner when it comes to bookkeeping and accounting, then QuickBooks makes a wonderful introduction into the world of accounting systems. However, there are some cases where QuickBooks isn't the best fit available and could prove to be more painful than it is worth. To avoid this experience, it is important to compare your needs against QuickBooks capabilities. Specifically, there are three key components that could make or break your relationship to QuickBooks.

Despite the fact that QuickBooks expanded its line of products to include QuickBooks Enterprise Solutions, QuickBooks is most often recommended for those looking to begin using an accounting system. Many consider QuickBooks to be easy to use and efficient considering the affordable price of the software compared to more advanced systems. It is pretty much unanimous across the internet that QuickBooks is a great introductory system, so if you are a smaller business and just getting started with accounting systems, then QuickBooks may be a great fit for you.

As your business grows, you can easily outgrow QuickBooks depending on the needs of your company. One of the issues that QuickBooks has is problems with managing a large and robust inventory. If your company sells a t-shirt design, it shouldn't be an issue. If your company sells hundreds of different t-shirt designs and you have to keep track of hundreds of products, then QuickBooks may not be the system for you. QuickBooks is great for lots of things, but for companies with a robust inventory, it can be a frustration.

Another issue that users have with QuickBooks is the limitation on users that QuickBooks seems to have in place. QuickBooks Pro lets you have three users on the system. QuickBooks Premier has a limit of five with a maximum of 25 users when you upgrade to the top tier plan (an expensive purchase). While three people should be more than enough for your needs as a small company, you can easily outgrow this limitation. If you already need access for more than five users, then you may consider skipping over QuickBooks, and instead, use a more advanced system for your accounting needs.

This is also true in regards to the file size limitations that QuickBooks has. As it is a great introductory tool, those using QuickBooks tend not to have overly large file sizes or data. As your business grows, so too does the file size that you are working with. Eventually, you will reach a size that is too large to work with within QuickBooks. When this happens, it is time to upgrade beyond QuickBooks. If you have a ton of data already and your file sizes are getting up there, then QuickBooks isn't a good option for you. Though if you have all that to begin with, then you have already grown beyond the scope of this book.

If you need more than three to five users or have a ton of inventory to manage, then QuickBooks is not a great choice for your business. However, if you are looking for your first accounting system, one that has plenty of features, an affordable price and is easy to use, then QuickBooks will be not just a good fit for you, but a great one.

The Advantages and Disadvantages of QuickBooks

By now you should have a good idea of whether or not QuickBooks is a fit for you. Even if QuickBooks fits your particular needs, you may still not be convinced that you need to transition to using a new accounting system. Making the switch to a new system can be a real pain and sometimes the advantages don't outweigh the annoyance of getting started. To close out this chapter, let's take a look at both the advantages and disadvantages of using QuickBooks.

While I believe that the advantages outweigh the disadvantages, I don't want to just present to you a one-sided story of why you should use this software. Instead, I want to give you the knowledge needed to make your own call. By the time you have finished with this section, and the chapter as a whole, you will have all the information you need to make an informed decision about QuickBooks.

Disadvantage: Can Be Hard to Get Started

When it comes to using QuickBooks, it can be pretty intimidating because there are so many options. With tabs for banking, sales, expenses, time, projects, workers, reports, taxes, accounting and more, there are a ton of different tabs to navigate around within QuickBooks and each is packed full of information for you about your finances. If you are a small business, many of the features of QuickBooks will be more advanced than you need, and it can be annoying to find the information you need when there is so much presented.

If you don't know what you are doing, then QuickBooks can take a long time to get set up. There are accounts to create, vendors to connect to, banks to connect with. You have to decide between several different versions of the QuickBooks software to find the one that is right for you. Getting all of this tackled and learning to navigate the QuickBooks interface isn't a whole lot of fun, and this can easily put off potential users. However, we'll be looking at how to navigate the interface in chapter three and spend the rest of the book learning how to get started. If you're reading this book, you have a leg up on this disadvantage.

Disadvantage: It Requires the Internet

Living on your own, you are unlikely to be without internet. If you are running a business, then the odds of being without are even greater. In our 21st century living, the internet is a necessity up there with food and housing. However, faulty routers, poor connection speeds , and ISP-errors can all knock out our connection to the rest of the wired world. This would also knock out our connection to QuickBooks Online because it requires an internet connection.

While most businesses will have no problem with QuickBooks requiring the internet, it is one of those requirements that doesn't seem like an issue until it is an issue. What I mean is that 99% of the time you need to access QuickBooks you will be able to, but there is always that 1% when you are having an issue with connecting to the internet but still need to get on QuickBooks. When this happens, you can't access it.

If you are having problems with your internet connection and still need to use QuickBooks, then you may be forced to head out to a public place with accessible internet such as a local library or coffee shop. Apart from going out somewhere to access the internet, your only other recourse is to wait for the internet to come back on so that you can use QuickBooks Online. If you are using the desktop version of QuickBooks, then this isn't an issue, however, Intuit has clearly focused their attentions on QuickBooks Online rather than the downloadable version.

Disadvantage: Upgrade Fees and Renewal Costs

In the next chapter, we will be looking at the types of plans available for using QuickBooks, but their prices often pop up around the internet as one of the negatives. While QuickBooks is cheaper than many of the accounting systems out there, which is why it is such a great system for those just learning how to bookkeep, the price tag can still be shocking to some.

If you buy a license for QuickBooks Pro, then you can expect to pay around $300. Intuit, the developer of QuickBooks, often has sales where you can purchase a license at a discounted rate. This license lets you use QuickBooks for three years. After three years, Intuit will stop supporting the program, though you can still use the software itself. If you want to backup your data with a QuickBooks Pro plan, then it will be another $10 a month. If you need phone support to help you through problems with the software, then that's $90 for a three month period. Annual upgrades to the latest build of the software will run you $300 again. All these costs make QuickBooks Pro more expensive than it first appears.

If you go with a QuickBooks Pro Plus account, then you will pay $300 a year but you will get access to all the annual upgrades, phone support, and data backups at no extra charge. This makes Pro Plus a great option and actually the way to go if you want to save money in the long run by avoiding all the little added fees that drain your bank account. While QuickBooks Online offers access to the latest version of QuickBooks with the monthly fee, add-ons and upgrades will still run you a lot of money depending on your needs.

Disadvantage: Lack of Professional Support

When it comes to support for QuickBooks, Intuit is severely lacking. The website Customer Service Scoreboard have ranged 956 companies. QuickBooks' customer support is ranked #643. Out of a possible 200 points, QuickBooks only scores 27.24, and 448 out of the 463 comments listed on the site are negative. Their attribute ratings aren't much better. Issue Resolution: 1.6 out of 10. Reachability: 2.2 out of 10. Cancellation: 2.0 out of 10. Friendliness: 3.8. Product Knowledge: 2.4.

One of the major issues relating to QuickBooks' support is the fact that it costs about $90 for three months of support if you don't have QuickBooks Pro Plus. That's a lot of money to drop on support that isn't very good. This is one of the biggest issues that people have with QuickBooks, and it is absolutely understandable. If you are paying a ton of money for an accounting system, you expect it to work and you expect to be able to get help if it isn't working. Unfortunately, this is not true with QuickBooks. It mostly works, but when it doesn't, it can be really annoying to figure out what is going wrong when you can't get good help.

But it isn't all bad. Because QuickBooks is such a widely used product, there are lots of people that have taken to forums and blog posts to share how they fixed the problems they ran into. Forums are particularly nice because you can describe your problem and ask for help and other QuickBooks users (plus support staff) can reply and help you out. The community is really good that way, and so while professional support is lacking, there is a ton of support available if you go looking for it.

Advantage: It Is Easy to Use Once You Know What You're Doing

The good news is that while QuickBooks can be hard to use when you are first getting started, it actually is pretty easy to use overall. If you know what you are doing, you will find QuickBooks to be a simple tool to use but a powerful one for your business. Learning to navigate is hard, but once you learn where everything is located, you'll be able to navigate with ease.

QuickBooks will take a lot off of your accounting and bookkeeping workload. You can connect financial information so it automatically pulls numbers into the system for you rather than you having to go through and add them in by hand. Many numbers will be crunched behind the scenes, and you can use the graphical displays that QuickBooks makes to figure out where your finances are with just a glance.

The hardest part of using QuickBooks is the starting, but once you get going, you will be surprised at how easy it actually is. Chapter three will help you to get started and learn your way around, and by the end of chapter five, you will have the knowledge necessary to go from a QuickBooks beginner to a QuickBooks apprentice.

Advantage: Access to Third-Party Apps

One of the coolest things about using QuickBooks is all the third-party apps that work with it. The QuickBooks website advertises over 270 accounting specific apps available to help you fine-tune your experience with their software. With so many options available, you can take some serious control over your QuickBooks experience and integrate most any other accounting software you happen to use.

We'll take a look at how we add these apps to our QuickBooks setup in chapter six, but here let's take a look at some of the more popular ones to get an idea for the kinds of apps that are out there. The most popular app is Expensify. This app helps in tracking expenses such as business receipts and mileage. When used with QuickBooks, it makes it really easy to see your expenses at a glance. TSheets has an app that integrates with QuickBooks to help you take care of employee management like tracking timesheets and creating timesheet reports so that your employees can use their time more productively. InvoiceSherpa's app connects to QuickBooks to help speed up your invoices and make sure you get paid faster. Cin7's app helps with managing sales channels, inventory and will update QuickBooks automatically with your latest purchases or sales.

These are just a couple of the third-party apps available for QuickBooks, but they give a good overview. They show that there are apps related to every part of your business, so if you need a helping hand to keep track of employees, then you can get an app for that. Want to speed up getting paid? There are apps for that. With over 270 different third-party apps, there are guaranteed to be apps that make your life easier.

Advantage: Directly Link to Online Bank Accounts

One of the most annoying parts of accounting is recording all the many different transactions that you do during the week. You buy, sell, buy, sell, rent, and buy some more, so by the end of the week, there is a ton of information you need to track and log. It is super easy to miss an entry when doing it by hand. Or, if you don't have a dedicated bank account for the business, you can easily forget what was a personal purchase and what was a business expense. Don't worry though, QuickBooks has you covered.

QuickBooks can integrate with over 18,000 different banks. Unless you use some kind of esoteric, mafia-owned bank, you can bet that QuickBooks works with whatever institute you bank with. This integration is easy to do, and we'll look at it in depth in chapter four. By integrating your bank with QuickBooks, you remove the need to manually enter every transaction. Instead, QuickBooks automatically downloads each transaction as they happen. If you have a business bank account, then it does everything for you. If you are working with a personal bank account for your business, then you will still have to go in and sort out the purchases that weren't business related, but otherwise, it saves you a ton of time and stress by automating your data entry for you.

Advantage: Accessible on All Platforms

You can download QuickBooks desktop and use it on your computer the same way you use the spider solitaire app. This is pretty cool, but where QuickBooks really shines is in just how accessible it is. It doesn't matter if you have a Mac or a PC, you can use QuickBooks. You don't want to download an application? Don't worry, you can access QuickBooks through your web browser.

What if you are out for lunch and realize you forgot to log some important information? They have you covered then too. Just whip out your phone and head over to the website to access the QuickBooks dashboard. It doesn't matter if it is on your computer or your phone, you can access QuickBooks from any device you need. This means that as long as you have a cell phone, you can always access your data and information.

Advantage: QuickBooks Is a Proven Product

One of the biggest advantages that QuickBooks has is the astonishing number of businesses and people that use it as their primary accounting system. There are over three million QuickBooks Online users around the world. That's a lot of users that find QuickBooks to be a beneficial tool in running their finances.

With so many users of the software, it has been tested again and again and has continued to be recommended as one of the best entry-level accounting and bookkeeping applications available today. These users actually serve to prove how powerful this product is. You don't get to three million users without providing a service that people love. Not only that, but you don't keep your numbers that high without constantly improving on the program and troubleshooting. Having so many users means that any bugs in the system will absolutely be caught. If Intuit missed them while programming the latest update, you can rest easy knowing that one of the three million users experienced it too and reported it to the company.

Not only is QuickBooks a proven product because of its userbase, but that userbase also helps each other out. As mentioned above, there is a lack of professional support from Intuit when it comes to QuickBooks, but it has actually served to build a better community, one that helps each other out online. QuickBooks has been proven useful by its userbase and improved on by them as well. The amount of information available online about QuickBooks is endless, so you know that any issues you have are ones that others have worked through and can help you with. This userbase is what makes QuickBooks stand out from the crowd of entry-level accounting programs.

Chapter Summary

- Your business should have an accounting system in order to collect the data necessary to tell if the company is growing or shrinking and so that you can make predictions about the future of your company.
- QuickBooks is best used by smaller companies or freelancers as there is a limitation on number of users, file sizes and inventory management that will leave larger companies frustrated.
- QuickBooks has a lot of information and can be hard to get started with when you are new to it.
- When you do get started, you will find that QuickBooks becomes easy to use and navigate.
- You must have an internet connection in order to use QuickBooks.
- There are over 270 accounting apps available from third-party developers to expand QuickBooks' functionality.
- Depending on the plan you purchase to use QuickBooks, there can be a bunch of charges and fees that can add up quickly.
- You can connect your bank account to QuickBooks in order to have purchases

automatically brought into the QuickBooks application rather than manually enter charges.

- The help support offered by Intuit for their QuickBooks program is considered one of the worst customer service experiences around.
- Whether you use a Mac or a PC, a computer or a cell phone, you can easily access QuickBooks on whatever platform you own.
- There are over three million QuickBooks users around the world. This means there are three million users testing out the software and spotting bugs and supporting each other online.

In the next chapter, you will learn which version of QuickBooks is best for you: QuickBooks Online or QuickBooks Desktop. You will learn all about the different plans that Intuit offers for QuickBooks to figure out what plans work best for the different types of businesses you run.

Pros
?
Cons

CHAPTER TWO

DECIDING WHICH QUICKBOOKS SOFTWARE TO USE

Now that you know if QuickBooks fits your needs, it is time to figure out which version of QuickBooks you want to use. In this chapter, we will look at the different plans available for QuickBooks to find out which is right for you and your particular type of business. This will be the last chapter of preparation before we get into the hands on, practical advice like setting up accounts and creating invoices.

There are different plans for QuickBooks depending on which version of the software you use: Online or Desktop. Both versions of the software have their purpose, so before you figure out which QuickBooks plan to choose, you must first decide which version of QuickBooks is right for you. Let's dive in.

QuickBooks: Online vs. Desktop

Both QuickBooks Online and QuickBooks Desktop have their uses, so it is unfair to proclaim one as being better than the other. That said, one of the clear differences that pops up when researching QuickBooks is the fact that Intuit is clearly betting that the cloud-based QuickBooks Online is the future of the software. While many websites (such as Fit Small Business) recommend using QuickBooks Online, there are still good reasons to pick Desktop over Online depending on the needs of your business.

QuickBooks Online is recommended most for those companies that are service-based rather than inventory-based. Likewise, Desktop is recommended for those with complex inventory tracking needs, because Desktop offers both first in first out tracking or tracking based on the average cost method. QuickBooks Online only offers first in first out tracking.

Besides the difference in costs, which we will look at next, there are some key differences between Online and Desktop with regards to their functionality. For example, QuickBooks Online doesn't require you to download or install anything. However, QuickBooks Online requires an internet connection while QuickBooks Desktop doesn't. QuickBooks Online makes up for this requirement by allowing access from any device, whereas QuickBooks Desktop only allows access from a single device and so works best for those that spend a lot of time in the office.

Since both QuickBooks Online and QuickBooks Desktop have features that the other doesn't, let's take a look at each in turn to see what unique features they offer. QuickBooks Online has a system to automatically backup data. Your information is automatically stored on Intuit's servers, which means you never have to worry about whether or not your data has been saved or whether it is protected. You can access your data anytime you want from a Mac or PC as all the information is stored in the cloud rather than on a single computer. A subscription to QuickBooks Online gets you access to technical support, though we've already seen that their support is not particularly good. However, a subscription also gives you access to the latest version of QuickBooks which, as we saw in the last chapter, means you can save hundreds of dollars on upgrading. Another nice feature of QuickBooks Online is that they include a sample file. This sample is great for seeing how QuickBooks looks when it is set up properly and can give you a risk-free environment to try out the software and figure out how to use it.

Using QuickBooks Desktop is quite a bit different from the QuickBooks Online service. For one, you have to install QuickBooks Desktop to your computer. This means that in order to access your data, you have to use the same platform that you installed it on. You aren't able to use your phone to check your QuickBook accounts when you use Desktop. However, you can use a hosting service (such as the one that QuickBooks Online uses) for an extra fee. This fee varies depending on the needs of the business and so you have to contact QuickBooks to get a quote. Because QuickBooks Desktop is not a cloud-based system, you will also have to manually backup and protect your information. You can get automatic backups from QuickBooks for $300 a year or you can use a system of your own choosing.

QuickBooks Desktop offers paid technical support as part of the yearly $300 required for automatic backups. You get 30 days of support free when you first install, after that you need to pay for it. Speaking of paying, you also need to pay for upgrades when you use QuickBooks Desktop. While typically QuickBooks Desktop is a one-time fee and QuickBooks Online is a monthly fee, the cost of upgrading can easily make QuickBooks Desktop a much more expensive option in the long run. However, QuickBooks Desktop offers a few different sample files across multiple industries which makes it easier to get a feel for how the system works. Desktop also has more options when it comes to tracking inventory and invoicing in batches. But the most compelling feature that QuickBooks Desktop has over QuickBooks Online is the industry-specific versions of the software that you can get. These include QuickBooks programs for general business, non-profits, contractors, professional services, manufacturing and wholesale companies, and retail companies.

When it comes to pricing, QuickBooks Online can run between $20 to $150 a month depending on which version of the software you get (simple start, essentials, plus, advanced). QuickBooks Desktop offers a one-time cost of $300 or $500 depending on the version you go with (Pro vs. Premier) or even $1040 a year for the enterprise version. While QuickBooks Online seems more expensive when compared to the one-time cost versions of Desktop, it is important to remember that QuickBooks Online offers access to their upgrades without any extra changes.

QuickBooks Online offers many useful features that would seem to be the best option. There are many accountants that have not made the switch from the desktop version, which has been around since the 1990s, to the online version. Fit Small Business considers this to be a mistake, and I would agree with them. QuickBooks Online makes it easier to get to your information, it automatically protects it at no added cost, and it gives access to the latest updates of the QuickBooks system. These features make QuickBooks Online the better option and with the growth of cloud-based systems, it is clear that Intuit's focus on QuickBooks Online reflects the future of QuickBooks.

Types of QuickBooks Plans + Features

Both QuickBooks Online and QuickBooks Desktop each have tiers of plans ranging from basic to comprehensive. In order to understand how each plan differs from the others, it is important that we take a moment to look at the features that come included in each plan. We will first explore QuickBooks Online and then take a look at the plans for QuickBooks Desktop.

QuickBooks Online: Self-Employed

Price: $10/month, half off for first three months.

QuickBooks Self-Employed is both the cheapest and the most bare-bones version of QuickBooks that you can get. As the title implies, it is designed with the self-employed user in mind, and so it is best used for those who are their own employee or run a business by themselves. As such, QuickBooks Self-Employed only allows one user. For those with limited accounting needs, QuickBooks Self-Employed can't be beat for the price. How about the features?

QuickBooks Self-Employed allows users to track miles automatically, or add them manually if they want with their smartphone, and categorize those trips as business or personal. This feature is great because the act of tracking miles will itself lead to a reduction in miles. QuickBooks reports an average of 45% reduction in travel budget this way.

Another included feature is the ability to track income and expenses. This is one of the key features you need out of your accounting system, and QuickBooks Self-Employed makes sure to include it. QuickBooks allows you to import transactions from your bank, credit card, PayPal and more. This means you can easily import your expenses and your income and let QuickBooks automatically sort them into the different tax categories they belong to. You can even take photos of your receipts and link them to the corresponding expense using your phone.

They say the only thing certain in life is death and taxes, so QuickBooks Self-Employed includes the ability to estimate your quarterly taxes automatically. Not only is it great because it lets you know what you owe before they are due, but it means less time wasted on taxes. No one enjoys taxes, which makes this feature a much appreciated addition to QuickBooks.

QuickBooks makes it easy to invoice, so easy that you can even do it from your smartphone. You can create partial invoices for each stage of a project, send clients reminders to pay, and even track the status of your invoices. Not only that, but it makes it even easier and quicker to get paid by including the ability to pay by credit card or bank transfer directly in the invoice itself.

Self-Employed includes the ability to run basic reports, which means that there are only four options available for reporting. You can create profit and loss reports, tax summaries, tax details, and receipts. For more options in reporting, you will have to upgrade to at least the Essentials package.

QuickBooks Self-Employed is the most straight forward of the services as far as advertising is concerned. Self-Employed is great service for self-employed individuals who are looking to begin tracking their finances easier.

QuickBooks Online: Simple Start

Price: $20/month, half off for first three months.

At twenty dollars a month, Simple Start is the lowest tier of "official" QuickBooks programs. Self-Employed is almost more of an off-shoot of the main QuickBooks products and this will be made more clear when we look at Essentials, Plus, and Advanced, all of which include the features of the tier before it and add more features on top of those.

There is some crossover between the features of Self-Employed and Simple Start. Most obvious of these is that both use basic reports rather than the advanced reports of Essentials, Plus, and Advanced. Simple Start can also capture receipts to connect to expenses, track those expenses, and track your income. After that, the two plans diverge.

While QuickBooks Self-Employed gives you the tools to estimate your quarterly taxes, Simple Start gives you the tools you need to maximize your tax deductions. You can easily share your books with your accountant or export any documents you need for taxes. Your income and expenses are sorted into tax categories like with Self-Employed. But rather than just providing an estimate of your quarterly taxes, QuickBooks Simple Start lets you get more involved with your taxes, and it will help you to maximize your deductions to really make every dollar spent go that little extra bit further.

Simple Start also offers the ability to send estimates. You can easily customize estimates to fit your brand and the needs of your business. You can get clients to sign estimates digitally using their computer or even their smartphone. Then you can take those estimates and quickly convert them into invoices. This makes it easy to work with clients through the early planning stages, the actual work and project management stages, and all the way through to getting paid.

QuickBooks Self-Employed seems to assume that you are providing a service to your customers. QuickBooks Simple Start begins the movement of the QuickBooks plans into the world of selling products. To help with this, QuickBooks Simple Start gives you the tools to track your sales and sales tax. They have a mobile card reader that will let you accept credit cards wherever you are, and they even automatically calculate sales tax on your invoices. As well as these features, they also allow you to connect to e-commerce tools like Shopify.

Self-Employed also makes it easy to keep up with all your 1099s. You can assign vendor payments to 1099 categories so that you can see who you've paid, when you paid them, as well as when you've been paid and who you were paid by. This information is then used to prepare and file your 1099s from within QuickBooks so you don't even have to the leave the app. These tools make it easy to keep up with all the legal paperwork required by the government.

Finally, QuickBooks Self-Employed is the first of the plans to introduce add-ons that you can purchase. When first signing up, these add-ons will be half price. You can add self service payroll to your plan for $35 a month, or $18 a month with the half off discount. Likewise, you can add full service payroll to your plan for $80 a month, or $40 with the half off discount. Both of these add-ons also require $4 a month for each employee you include.

The self-service payroll allows you to pay employees and contractors anytime you choose with free 24-hour direct deposit and unlimited pay schedules. You can easily pay and file federal or state payroll taxes without ever having to leave QuickBooks, and you can even print and file any W2s required at the end of the year. The full-service payroll offers all these features, plus it gives you access to professionals who will set up, file, and pay your payroll taxes for you. Full service also allows your employees to get their money even faster with same day direct deposit.

QuickBooks Simple Start is best for those who run a company on their own. Simple Start is really more of an expansion of the features in QuickBooks Self-Employed to give you more control over your finances.

QuickBooks Online: Essentials

Price: $40/month, half off for first three months.

QuickBooks Essentials has everything included in Simple Start, including the options for payroll add-ons, however it includes a couple new features that may be of interest to those who run companies with multiple employees or time-based payments.

The first major difference between QuickBooks Essentials and the previous plans is that Essentials offers you the ability to have multiple users. Essentials lets you have up to three users. This means that you can invite your accountant to access your books to easily collaborate. You can give employees access to specific features so that you can pick what each user has the ability to change. This is great for reducing errors. Error reduction is further reduced by auto-syncing across all users. This way you and your employees are working off the same data rather than each having their own version of the numbers.

Essentials also lets you manage your bills through the QuickBooks platform. You can track the status of your bills, record any payments you've made, and set up recurring payments so you never miss a deadline. You can pay multiple vendors or bills at the same time and can even create checks to print off.

The final feature added in Essentials is the ability to track time. This is great for those companies that are paid (or pay their employees) by the hour rather than by project. QuickBooks Essentials lets you track billable hours by client or by employee and automatically takes these numbers and adds them to invoices. You can enter your numbers yourself, or you can give your employees access to enter them themselves. You can even integrate with TSheets, another software designed for use with QuickBooks, to make time tracking easier.

QuickBooks Essentials best fits a small business, one that needs to track income, expenses, and accounts receivable in addition having to pay suppliers and keep track of money heading in more than one direction.

QuickBooks Online: Plus

Price: $70/month, half off for the first three months.

Plus is the most popular of the QuickBooks Online packages. It's also the second most expensive and only adds a few features that weren't included in Essentials. Plus is definitely best for a company that needs multiple users and requires inventory-focused features.

QuickBooks Plus offers access for up to five users, expanding on Essentials three. Again, this is a feature that is clearly aimed towards businesses that have a number of employees. Not every employee needs access, only those responsible for the finances.

A new feature that Intuit added recently is the ability to track project profitability. This feature lets you see all your projects from a bird's eye view so that you can easily track the cost of labor, all the payroll information, and the expenses that each project accues. This view lets you see how profitable your projects are at a quick glance.

The final addition to Plus is the ability to track inventory. Plus allows you to track your products and the cost of goods. You can also set it to give you a notification whenever your inventory is starting to run low. This lets you see which of your items are the most popular. You can also create purchase orders and manage vendors with these features.

While Plus only adds three extra features, don't forget that it includes all of the features from Essentials and Simple Start. Plus is the first of the

QuickBooks plans with inventory tracking features, and so it best fits a smaller business that deals in products or services that will benefit from tracking.

QuickBooks Online: Advanced

Price: $150/month, half off for first three months.

Advanced is the final and most expensive of the QuickBooks Online plans. It's also the newest of the plans and is clearly aimed at large businesses. While QuickBooks is most often recommended for smaller business, Advanced is an attempt to offer larger companies the tools they need to keep QuickBooks as their primary accounting system.

Advanced includes everything in Essentials. Where Essentials allows up to five users, Advanced offers twenty-five. This massive jump is obviously more than most small companies will ever need but can easily be too few depending on how massive your company is. However, if you are looking to get started with QuickBooks, then it is safe to assume that twenty-five users is a little bit more than you need at this point in time.

Advanced introduces smart reporting powered by Fathom™. Fathom™ is a tool for making more involved and reactive finance reports. It typically costs around $500 a year, but is included with the Advanced plan at no extra cost. It helps you to make customizable performance reports by using clear and simple visuals. This helps you to see how profitable the company has been, how and where cash is flowing, and many other important statistics.

Another new feature is accelerated invoicing. Intuit claims that accelerated invoicing lets you create invoices 37% faster. You can import hundreds of invoices at the same time. It only takes you a few clicks to duplicate invoices and alter them slightly. This allows you to make your invoices super quick so that you're not losing time creating invoices one at a time.

With up to twenty-five users, it is important that you make sure sensitive data isn't falling into the wrong hands. Advanced offers customer user permissions to help you keep your data safe and secure. You can set the limitations of what each user can see, that way your employees work only with the information you have delegated to them. You can set up use permissions around deposits, expense reports, sales transitions, and more.

The final feature of Advanced is what they call premium care with Priority Circle. This means that you can connect with a customer success manager that has been dedicated to you. This manager is available to you for whenever you run into an issue that you need help with. Their job is to help you to resolve issues that you may run into, and it even offers access to a self-paced online QuickBooks training course that has a value of

$2000. All of this makes QuickBooks Advanced the best online option for large companies.

If your business is starting to grow to a larger size and you have complex needs that you need your accounting system to meet, then it is time to use QuickBooks Advanced. While it is the most expense plan, it is much more robust than the other versions and well worth it if you feel it would meet your needs.

QuickBooks Desktop: Pro 2019

Price: $299.95, one-time fee.

Many of the features of QuickBooks Desktop are available with QuickBooks Online. Some are almost exactly the same, while others have slight differences. In order to get a clear understanding of these features, we will be looking at them all. This means that several of these features will be familiar to those who read the previous section.

You get the same income and expense tracking that you got with Online, but now when it comes time to run reports on those finances, you have access to over a hundred different kinds of reports. You can also invoice, send estimates, and track sales tax from QuickBooks Desktop Pro 2019.

Another feature of QuickBooks Desktop is the inventory tracking. While inventory tracking wasn't brought into QuickBooks Online until the $75 a month Plus package, it is included in every version of Desktop from Pro to Enterprise. You are also able to set up some huge lists with Desktop; Pro and Premier allow up to 145, 000 items per list while Enterprise will allow you to have more than a million.

Speaking of keeping track of things, Desktop Pro comes with a time tracking component. This allows you to keep track of your billable hours and the amount of time your employees have worked. Pro 2019 allows you up to three users, though each user requires you to buy an additional licence. You still have to get an add-on to be able to pay your employees through the QuickBooks software, though you do have access to paying 1099 contractors with the base software.

You can get an upgrade to Plus, which in this case means you get access to unlimited customer support, data backups, and upgrades. Also available as an add-on is remote hosting, which allows you to store your data on the cloud so that you can access it anywhere. Or, in other words, it lets you use Desktop as if it was Online.

There are also a bunch of features that have just been added to the 2019 edition of QuickBooks Desktop. These include getting real-time information on invoices and the ability to expedite collections to keep up with cash flow. You can transfer credits from customer jobs with the click of a button now. You can also view unpaid bills from vendors to more easily manage the payments you are making. Another new feature added to the 2019 edition is the ability to reliably reduce file sizes without risking any loss of data. Plus, 2019 makes it easier to track employee sick time and vacation days.

QuickBooks Desktop: Premier 2019

Price: $499.95, one-time fee.

Premier 2019 offers all the same features as Pro 2019, however they expanded a few things. Premier offers access for up to five users, though each user requires you to buy an additional licence. Premier also offers the same add-ons as Pro: an upgrade to Plus, the ability to pay employees, and remote hosting.

The features that are unique to Premier over Pro are their forecasting tools and their industry specific features. The forecasting tools allow you to forecast progress in either dollars or percentages by using the previous years' numbers or imputing your own. You can even create forecasts by customer.

The industry specific tools are designed around six key industries: general contractor, manufacturing and wholesale, nonprofit, professional services, retail, and general business. These tools are what sets QuickBooks Desktop apart from QuickBooks Online.

For nonprofits there are tools to create end-of-year donation statements, create 990 forms, and run donor contribution summary reports. General contracting tools include the ability to create jobs by vendor, create job estimates, track change orders, and analyze job profitability. On the manufacturing and wholesale side of things, you get the ability to track inventory reorders point by vendor to track and set the optimal levels for your inventory. You can also track profitability by product and easily prioritize the orders you've got. Professional services include tools to track unbilled time and expenses, set different billing rates by client, service or employee, and analyze the client and project profitability. Going with the retail tools, you can easily track sales results, keep up with inventory tracking, and run monthly profit and loss reports against each other. The general business tools are those that QuickBooks typically uses.

QuickBooks Desktop: Enterprise 19.0

Price: $1155/year.

The most expensive of all the QuickBooks plans, Enterprise includes the most features. It is still a desktop-based system and so if you want access to your files remotely you will have to purchase the remote hosting add-on. However, despite this limitation, Enterprise is the most powerful of the QuickBooks applications.

Along with everything included in the Premier 2019 package, Enterprise 19.0 offers mobile inventory barcode scanning, access to QuickBooks Priority Circle, enhanced pick, pack and shipping, and it increases the maximum users to 30 (though you still must purchase an extra license for each user).

The first of these additions, mobile inventory barcode scanning, gives you the ability to prioritize which sales orders are taken care of first and to create customer pick lists in your warehouses and send those lists to barcode scanners. It also gives you the ability to scan inventory and update sales orders in real-time, making this the ultimate package for retail-based businesses.

The QuickBooks Priority Circle is a loyalty program that was built to give you access to a dedicated customer success manager. You can call this manager whenever you have any questions about QuickBooks products. It also gives you access to product training for both you and your employees and to expert care from product specialists over the phone or online chat.

The enhanced pick, pack and ship features are made to help you to streamline sales order fulfilment with better accuracy. You can manage the end-to-end workflow from a central dashboard, send items to the packer with a single click, and print out shipping labels from most of the major carriers without ever leaving the QuickBooks application.

Chapter Summary

- QuickBooks Online lets you access the QuickBooks software from any device with web browsing capabilities for a recurring monthly fee.
- QuickBooks Desktop requires that you install the QuickBooks application onto a computer, and then you can only access your QuickBooks data when using that computer.
- The QuickBooks Desktop application offers better inventory tracking services and industry specific versions, but it is clear that Intuit is pushing QuickBooks Online as their primary interest.
- QuickBooks Self-Employed is the cheapest version of the QuickBooks Online system and is designed with the freelancer in mind.
- QuickBooks Simple Start offers a bunch of the QuickBooks features for a reasonable price, though it is still a simplified version of the QuickBooks program.
- QuickBooks Essentials offers everything you need to track employee time and keep on top of your bookkeeping and accounting while keeping a reasonable price.
- QuickBooks Plus adds inventory tracking tools to the QuickBooks software while also

increasing the number of users that can access the system.

- QuickBooks Advanced is the most expense of the QuickBooks Online systems and is clearly designed for larger companies, at which point many will have moved on to more advanced accounting software.
- QuickBooks Desktop Pro 2019 is the lowest of the QuickBooks Desktop applications but gives access to most of the features that QuickBooks uses.
- The primary addition to QuickBooks Desktop Premier 2019 is the industry specific tools that have extra features designed to service six key industries: general business, professional services, retail, manufacturing and wholesale, general contractors, and nonprofits.
- QuickBooks Desktop Enterprise 19.0 costs a yearly fee rather than a one-time cost unlike other desktop versions of QuickBooks, but Enterprise 19.0 includes access to the QuickBooks Priority Circle loyalty program, inventory barcode scanning, and enhanced tools for shipping products.
- The QuickBooks Priority Circle is a loyalty program that sets members up with their own dedicated customer success manager, offers product training for your business, and gives

you access to help from QuickBooks product specialists.

In the next chapter, you will learn how to get a QuickBooks account and how to navigate around the QuickBooks Online interface. You will also learn and create your accounts within QuickBooks. Along with accounts, you will set up your first customers and input your first vendors.

CHAPTER THREE

GETTING STARTED USING QUICKBOOKS

Now that you know which version of QuickBooks is right for you, it is time to begin setting up an account and learning how to navigate through the various menus and pages. We'll first look at the requirements you need for the software, how to make an account, how to navigate the program, and then we'll close out the chapter by setting up our first accounts, customers and vendors.

Requirements for QuickBooks

While QuickBooks Online can be accessed from anywhere with an internet connection, QuickBooks Desktop requires a system that can run the software. We'll look at those requirements here first before we turn our attention over to starting an account.

In order to use QuickBooks Desktop, you must first be using a Windows computer. Intuit claims that you have to use a native Windows operating system.

This means that you can't use a Mac with the software, nor can you use an emulated version of Windows such as you can create on a Mac or Linux system. Furthermore, if you have purchased the add-on to allow for remote hosting, you must use Internet Explorer 11 in order to access this information. Mac users must use QuickBooks Online as it is the only way to get access to the application.

For this reason, we will be exploring how to use QuickBooks Online, rather than the desktop version of the software. This will allow you to make use of the information within, regardless of whether you use Windows, Mac or Linux. Not only that, but it is clear that Intuit is really pushing and expanding QuickBooks Online to be their flagship product to make the best use of the move towards cloud-based software and data storage.

To access QuickBooks, you must first create an account with Intuit. Setting up your account is easy. If you have a Google account you can even have Google fill out the first step for you. To fill it out on your own is as easy as signing up for anything these days. You will first enter your email address, which will also double as your user ID. Enter your first and last name. They recommend that you enter a mobile phone number, but this isn't a requirement. Finally, enter a password and click "one more step." You will be asked to confirm your email address after signing up, and now is as good of a time as any. To do this, you just need to go to your email, find the message sent by Intuit/QuickBooks, open it, and click the confirmation link. The next step is to enter your credit or debit card number. Intuit accepts Visa, MasterCard, Discovery, and American Express. After filling out your payment options, you are now a proud subscriber to the QuickBooks plan you have chosen.

After you have gotten through setting up your Intuit account and your payment information, they will begin to ask you questions about your business. First they ask for your name, which is easy enough. Then they ask how long you have been in business. This question is designed for QuickBooks to learn a little bit about you and your needs. If you've been in business for more than a year then it will make the assumption that there is information you will need to import into the system. On this page, you will also see a button you can check to indicate that you have been using QuickBooks Desktop and will be importing data from there into QuickBooks Online.

Once you have clicked next, you will be asked what you would like to do in QuickBooks. You have eight options ranging from sending and tracking invoices, through to paying your employees and tracking your retail sales. These options are designed as a way to help you get started using QuickBooks. You can select as many or as little as you want. When you select them, QuickBooks then sends you articles and information about those processes. Feel free to select whatever you want, though the articles that Intuit have made available are rather sparse and we will be covering each bit of this information in greater depth in this book. Once you click set, you will be taken to the QuickBooks Dashboard and be introduced to the application proper.

Navigating QuickBooks

When you first get into QuickBooks, there is absolutely no information. If you are looking online at different guides, you will notice that they show the dashboard with a ton of information like colorful graphs in the profit and losses and expenses sections. However, this information has to be put into QuickBooks first. What you will see on a new account is a series of steps for you to take to get started, such as connecting your bank or creating your first invoice. We will get to these in just a moment. First, we need to figure out what we're even looking at.

The first page that you see anytime that you open up QuickBooks is the dashboard. The dashboard shows you a summary of your information. If you just need to pop in to check a balance or the like, then you will only have to open the dashboard to get the information you need. You will see headings for invoices, expenses, profit and loss, bank accounts, and sales. These give you the numbers and useful graphics to see how everything is going. They are designed to show you information for the last 30 days, but each has a drop-down menu to the right of their title which you can click to set the time frame you are interested in. All of them except for the bank accounts section have this feature. This section shows you the latest activity from your connected bank accounts. You need to review the transactions in this section in order to approve them being brought into QuickBooks. This is especially useful if you do not have a separate bank account for your business and personal finances. Also, on this page, to the right just above the bank accounts section, is a switch you can toggle labelled privacy. This allows you to hide the information on the dashboard, which can be good if you are in a public place or suddenly have someone stop by and you don't want them to see all your information.

On the left side of the screen is a vertical menu with a bunch of different options: customers, suppliers, employees, transactions, reports, taxes, and apps. Each of these options will take you to a different page, and this is your primary way of navigating around QuickBooks. Please be aware that these navigational options have changed in the past. For example, banking used to be its own section but is now under the transactions section.

The first page we'll look at is the transactions page, under which are several options. Click on banking. On the top of this page you will see any bank accounts that you have connected to your QuickBooks account. Clicking on one of these accounts brings up all the transaction information that you have approved for QuickBooks. Transactions show the date, description, the payee (if there is one), the category it has been sorted into, and how much money was spent or received in that transaction. If you have ever used online banking or a platform like PayPal, then this section will look quite familiar. You can add accounts from this page, too. If you look at the top of the page, you will see horizontal menu with two options: banking and bank rules. You should see the banking option underlined because that is the page the side menu opens up to. The bank rules tab allows you to automate the categorizing of transactions based on rules that you input; this allows you to automate regular transactions such as monthly bills.

Next up is the sales page. When you open up the page you will see a chart of all your sales, invoices, and the like. These are sorted by date and include the customer they are sent to, the invoice number, due dates, age of invoice, the balance, the total, and their status. The top of the page tells you some information at a glance, like how many invoices are overdue and how much is left owing, or how many have been paid and how much money they total. From the horizontal menu on the top, you can get to the invoices, customers, or products and services tabs to set up information about each of those topics. We will be looking more at these as we go forward.

Clicking on the expenses page will take you to another chart. This one tracks dates, types, numbers, payees, categories and totals of the various expenses that you have accrued. You can easily add a new transaction by clicking the green button to the top right and you can filter the list using the drop-down menu to the left.

From the side menu, click on the suppliers' section to pull up information on the vendors you work with. Clicking on this tab changes the page to one that looks a lot like the sales page. On the top, you will see some numbers at a glance that have been color-coded to help you tell what each of them are such as paid or unpaid vendor bills. Below you have yet another chart, though this one lists vendor names, phone numbers, email addresses, and the open balance with each company. The new transaction button from the previous tab is now an add new vendor button so that you can get all the vendors you work with and their contact information onto one easy-to-read page.

The employees page is similar to the vendors section. Here, you can add employees and see a list of their names, numbers and email addresses. Likewise, at the top you have options to go in and add any contractors you work with. The reports page gives you the various kinds of reports that you can make. The taxes page shows you all your tax information, payments, balances, taxable sales versus gross sales, and all of the information you need to handle that aspect of your business.

The final options are accounting and my accountant. In the accounting section you will find the chart of accounts section where you can keep track of transactions and more. The my accountant page is designed to be used by your accountant. You can use it to communicate with your accountant, see requests they have for any information they need you to provide them. From a request, you can comment or directly link documents to share. These pages are great for in-company accountants or working with out of company accountants.

Those are the main tabs from the sidebar menu, however there are also some buttons that you'll see at the top of the page. To your top left you will see a question mark in a circle. This is the help menu which you use to access useful articles and information to help you avoid getting lost in all the different pages and information in front of you. The plus icon is called the quick create menu. From this menu, you can easily create customers, invoices, payments, vendors, and all sorts of different elements. You can create these elements by navigating to their proper page using the sidebar menu and the horizontal tabs at the top of each page, or you can use the quick create menu to create them from any QuickBooks page you happen to be on.

The gear icon in this top section pulls up a mini-menu similar to the quick create menu. This menu gives you links to your account settings, to set up new users, and to quickly access your chart of accounts or your products and services. It also has links to your profile, a list of tools you can quickly access such as importing or exporting data, or access to your budgeting.

The account settings option opens up a popup with a ton of options in it. You will see a sidebar to the left with tabs for company, sales, expenses and advanced. Here you can edit information about your company and customize your preferences regarding sales or expenses. The advanced tab will give you even more customization options. These can be quite advanced and well beyond the understanding of a beginner. You don't need to mess with these, especially to begin with. But as you learn more about your company's needs and how to use QuickBooks, you will likely find yourself changing these more often.

That is how you navigate through QuickBooks and find where all your information is hidden throughout it. There are a ton of different tabs and pages, and so when we look at how we tackle setting up accounts, customers, create invoices and the like, we will cover where each particular piece of information is found again. It can be easy to get lost at this stage when you're just learning where stuff is, but as you begin to use each of the sections, you will grow more comfortable. In no time, you'll be navigating through QuickBooks like a pro.

Setting Up Accounts

In order to use QuickBooks, you are going to have to set up your chart of accounts. This is the foundation of your accounting system, and everything you do in QuickBooks will be built upon the chart of accounts. Every transaction you bring into QuickBooks is categorized and sorted by QuickBooks through the chart of accounts so that the program can generate your income statements and all the other financial statements you will be using.

When you setup your QuickBooks account, QuickBooks will automatically create accounts for you to begin with. These are typically an accounts receivable, accounts payable, inventory assets, sales tax payable, and retained earnings. If you need to track anything that doesn't fit into one of these lists, then you are going to have to create a new account. These accounts will cover all the major categories that you are going to run into, but you can personalize by adding your own lists. If you work with people on an international level and you want to track how much you are making or losing due to conversion rates, then you could create a new account list to track it. Or if you want to track how much you lose in service charges then there's another list you can make. Likewise, if your company is service-based and doesn't sell any products then you will want to delete the inventory asset list because it is irrelevant to your needs.

When you are setting up a new account, there are several categories that you can assign it: assets, liabilities, owner's equity, income, and expenses. Assets are used for accounts such as inventory. Liabilities could be used for things like your mortgage or auto loans. Owner's equity is used for accounts like retained earnings or contributed capital. Income is straight forward, you could use this one to track your sales whether from products or services. Expenses is used to track accounts such as office supply costs or payroll. Assets, liabilities and owner's equity will appear within the balance sheet while income and expenses are used to calculate your profit and loss statements.

Let's create, edit and delete a new chart of accounts list so that you can see how to tackle every step of working within our chart of accounts. First, we need to make a new account.

In order to create a new account, we need to navigate to the chart of accounts section. You can do this by clicking on the accounting button on the sidebar menu or by clicking on the gear icon in the top right corner and then clicking on chart of accounts. Once it's open, go ahead and click the green button that says "new" in the upper right corner. This opens up the account creation form. Here, you will pick which type of account you want to create and add a name and description of the account. You will also have to select the detail type. The detail type will be based on the account type that you select, and below the detail type selecting menu, you will see a description of what the type you have selected is used for. Click the save button and you've got yourself a new account.

If you want to modify the account, then you will need to first find it in your chart of accounts section. Once you have found the account you want to modify, you then click the drop arrow next to the account and select edit. This will pull up the same account creation form that you saw when you made the account. In here you can edit and change the name or description of the account. You can also change the category type. However, if you have already entered transactions into the account, then changing the category type could mess up your financial statements going forward.

Finally, to delete an account is just as easy. Once you have found the account you want to delete, you will click that drop arrow again, but this time you will select delete instead of edit. This will bring up a popup that asks if you are sure you want to delete the account. Select yes and then the account is deleted. Remember, there is no way to undo a delete. So, if you delete an account you meant to keep or you forgot to get information off the account before deleting it, you are going to lose that data and have to input it all over again.

Creating Your First Customers

With the chart of accounts out of the way, we move our attention to those our business serves: the customers. If your business is in the habit of sending invoices to customers, then you are going to want to set up customers within QuickBooks. This will allow you to send our invoices quicker in the future as it collects all the information you need for QuickBooks to take care of the delivery of the invoices. When you make invoices later on, you will see a drop-down menu from which you can select customers from the list you set up in this step. Not only will it be faster to send off invoices but QuickBooks will also track sales by customer so that you can see exactly what each customer is purchasing and how much money they are bringing the company. We can add customers into QuickBooks manually or through a CSV file. We'll take each of these in turn.

In order to add customers manually, we need to first navigate over to the customers page. To find it, you will first click on invoicing from the side menu and then click the customers tab on the top menu. On the top right of the screen, you should see a new customers button. Click it and you will see a customer information form pop up. Here, you fill out all the information about your customer: title, name, email, the company they work for, how you want their name displayed, their phone number, website, what name is printed on checks and invoices, and their billing and shipping addresses. You don't need to fill out every single section, only those that are marked with an asterisk. Everything else is based on the information you have. So if you only ask customers for their name and email, you would only fill out their name and their email.

Down where you fill out their billing and shipping addresses, you will see a series of tabs: address, notes, tax info, payment and billing, and attachments. Let's look at payment and billing first as it is the most important of them. In this section, you can set the customer's preferred payment method like cash or credit, as well as their preferred delivery method for invoices like email or mail. In this section, you can also set an opening balance in case you have a history with the customer before logging them in QuickBooks. What's more, you can also set up payment terms. These are used to set up when an invoice for that customer is due. Typically, you will have a base payment term, say thirty days. This means that every customer will owe their payment within thirty days of receiving an invoice from you. But if you have a customer that you know well and offer a longer payment window, then you can change their payment terms in this section. This will leave the terms for your customers the same, except for this specific customer.

What about those other tabs mentioned above? The notes section is straight forward enough. It allows you to enter any information about the client you want. This could be more information about their account with you and anything unique about it or even just a simple description of who they are so that you don't forget. QuickBooks doesn't use any of the information in the notes section and the customer can't see it, so it is purely for information disseminated within your company. The tax information section is where you make a note of the customer's resale permit information. The attachments section allows you to upload files to the customer's profile. If you have important information (say the customer has provided you with an outline for the job they are hiring you for), you can upload it in this section to have easy access to it.

Make sure you look over and double-check the information you've added. If everything looks right, then you can go ahead and save the customer. You've now created your first customer within QuickBooks. If you already have a bunch of customers, the easiest thing to do is add them into an Excel or CSV file and then import their information into QuickBooks using that file.

In order to do this, you want to first open up Excel to create a spreadsheet of your customers. You should have columns for customer names, company names, email addresses, telephone numbers, and billing and shipping addresses. Now, you don't need every one of these. For example, if you company doesn't ship any products, then you won't need the shipping information. First and last name, email, the billing address, and the phone number make up the most important data that you want to capture. Create a new row for each customer and fill out this information. Make sure that each row follows the same format; if you log the first row as last name, first name, email address, then you will want to log all the following rows in that same order. Save your spreadsheet somewhere you can easily find it on your computer and head back over to QuickBooks.

On the customer's page you will see a drop arrow next to the new customer button you clicked previously. From this drop menu you will see an option to import customers. Click it, and it will open the import form. Uploading is done in three steps. The first step is to click the browse button. This will pop up an explorer window where you can navigate to the folder you saved the spreadsheet in. Once you find the spreadsheet, click it and okay the upload. The next step is to map your data. In this section, you connect the columns you set up with their corresponding entry in QuickBooks. Your fields do not need to match those that QuickBooks provides. For example, QuickBooks refers to the street that customers live on. If you have named your "roads" rather than "streets" then you won't have a problem. You click the drop menu under your field column and select roads where QuickBooks has listed street. Do this for all your columns so that QuickBooks knows which information to put where.

Next, you will be brought into the third and final step, which is where you will want to double check all the information before you commit to importing. It will show you all the customers that you have setup and show you where all the information has mapped to. Names, companies, phone numbers, all of that will be here and you will see the information you put in your spreadsheet now in QuickBooks. If something is wrong, then you can adjust it on this step without having to go back and remap the whole thing. When you are satisfied that everything is correct, you can then click import. It'll take a second, but QuickBooks will let you know when the import is done.

If you want to edit a customer's information that is already in your system, navigate to the customer page and click on their name. It will be a blue hyperlink that opens up all their information like when you first created them. To delete a customer, you need to have not used them in a transaction before. If you have ever used them in a transaction, then you will be unable to delete them as they are now tied in with all your information. But if you don't want to work with a customer anymore, then you can use the drop menu next to their name on the customers page to select the make inactive option. This option hides the customer and their information from the customer page so that they aren't shown anymore. However, this allows QuickBooks to keep all the necessary information it needs for finance records and bookkeeping.

Setting Up Vendors

Setting up vendors is a lot like setting up customers. When you have a vendor added to QuickBooks, it will speed up your ability to pay bills and it will help you by tracking expenses by vendor. Like with customers, we can add vendors automatically or by importing a spreadsheet file, and we'll look at both options.

The first step to adding new vendors is to navigate to the vendors section of QuickBooks. This is found by clicking on expenses on the side menu and then clicking the vendors tab found on the top menu. Once you are there, you will click the new vendor button, which will again be found to the top right of the vendors list. Like with customers, this will pop up a form, though this one will be slightly different. The first thing you will notice is that much of the information that was spread out for customers is now directly in front of you. You will fill out the company's name, what you want the display name to be, their email, phone number, fax number, and address. If you are working with an individual vendor, rather than a company as a whole, you can include a first and last name here. You will notice that attachments and notes are included on this page, these act just like they did with customers, only now you don't have to hunt for them under their own tabs. You will also see payment terms within this section, as well as options for opening balance, account numbers, business ID numbers, and billing rates. Of importance here is the business ID number. You will need to get the tax ID or social security number from any vendors you work with because this is necessary for the 1099 tax forms which QuickBooks can help you to generate. There is also a box below the business ID number section which you can check off to have QuickBooks track the vendors to include on 1099 reports.

Once you have filled out the information on this form, you should review everything before you save it. You will now see the vendor included on the vendors page as part of the list. If it is your first vendor, it will be the only one. If you already work with several vendors but haven't gotten them into the QuickBooks system, then you may want to import all your vendors at once by using a spreadsheet. Like we did with customers, we will open up Excel and log each vendor's information as a separate row. You will want to include the business names, first and last names if you use them, emails, phone numbers, remit to addresses, and any other information you want to log about them. Save this spreadsheet somewhere you can easily find it during the next step.

On QuickBooks you will want to navigate to the vendors page if you aren't there already. From the drop menu next to "new vendor" you will find the import vendors option. Clicking this will take you to a similar three step import process that you saw when importing customers. Click the browse button and find the vendor spreadsheet you just saved. Upload it and move to the map data step. Here, you will see a QuickBooks online field column to the left and a column called "your field" to the right. Line up your fields with the QuickBooks fields. Once you have sorted through all the fields you have in your spreadsheet, you will move to the next step. Here, you can review all your data to make sure everything is correct before you upload. You are able to edit and alter any of the sections during this step so that you can make minor adjustments and fixes without having to reupload the spreadsheet file or map the data all over again. When you are satisfied, you okay the step and let QuickBooks import all your vendors. Now you should see all of your vendors on the vendors page.

If you want to edit a vendor, you will click on their name from the vendors page and find the edit button. This will open up the vendor creation window but with all the information of that vendor already filled out. If you want to delete a vendor, then you run into the same issue we found when deleting customers. You cannot delete a vendor who you have had a transaction with. They are now a part of your financial records and to delete them would mess up the whole system. So rather than allow you to delete a vendor, QuickBooks lets you hide them. To do this, you need to click on the name of the vendor you want to hide. From the window that pops up, you will want to find the edit button again, which should be in the corner of the screen. On the bottom left of the edit form, you will see a button to make the vendor inactive. Clicking this will hide the vendor. However, if you still have an outstanding balance with the vendor, then QuickBooks will pop up a warning to let you know that making them inactive will force a transaction to adjust the outstanding balance to zero. You can agree or deny this request. If you agree, the transaction will be made and the vendor hidden. If you deny the request, then no transaction will be made and the vendor will remain visible.

Chapter Summary

- While QuickBooks Online can be accessed from any device with an internet connection, QuickBooks Desktop requires a computer running Windows as its operating system.
- You must have an account to use QuickBooks Online, but creating an account with software company Intuit is a quick and simple process.
- Everytime we open Quickbooks, we are opening up to the dashboard. The dashboard is a single page that gives an overview of your account.
- To the left-hand side of the dashboard, and all subsequent pages, is the sidebar menu. From here you can navigate to the various pages within QuickBooks.
- The transactions page is where you will find your bank information like the transactions you need to sort into QuickBooks and those you already have.
- Also located under the transaction section is the sales page. This takes you to a chart of all your sales and your invoices.
- The expenses tab, still under transactions, takes you to a chart that tracks the various expenses that the company has paid or is left to be paid.

- The employees page lets you add and track your employees and you can enter payroll from here if you purchased the payroll add-on.
- You are able to generate reports from the report page and find all your tax information under the taxes page.
- On the top of any page in QuickBooks, you will find the quick create button. Click this cross shaped button to open a menu from which you can directly create any element you are looking for.
- Next to the quick create button is a gear shaped button that will open up options to edit your profile and change your settings.
- When you first sign up for QuickBooks, it automatically generates some accounts for your chart of accounts.
- You create a new account from the chart of accounts page. Here, you can create an account, edit or delete them.
- Every account you make needs to have a category like assets, income, expenses or the like. This way, QuickBooks knows which accounts to use for the calculations it makes behind the scenes.
- Creating customers is necessary so that you can send invoices and get detailed information on how much a particular client is worth.

- To create a customer, you must navigate to the customer creation form and fill out their name, billing info, shipping address and any other pieces of information that QuickBooks marks with an asterisk.
- When creating a customer, you have the option to create a memo. Anywhere you see the option for a memo, that means only those within your QuickBooks account can see this note. The customer will never know it exists.
- When creating a customer, you can set their payment terms to be unique to them. The payment terms represent how many days the customer has to get back to you with an invoice.
- You can quickly add multiple customers or vendors by uploading a spreadsheet with them all listed out in it. This lets you bring in a lot of customers at one time and sort them easily to quickly get them inside QuickBooks.
- Setting up a vendor is a lot like setting up a customer. Find their page on QuickBooks, click the add button and then fill out their information. You will need to get a tax ID or a social security number from any vendors that you work with.
- You can use check a box when creating a vendor to have QuickBooks track the vendor you have added to include them on any 1099 reports you create.

In the next chapter, you will learn how to use QuickBooks to take care of all your basic bookkeeping needs. You will learn how to send your first invoice and create credit memos to cover any mistakes that might arise. You'll also learn how to pay your employees using QuickBooks to make your payroll experience as smooth as possible. We'll also look at how we keep track of our bank accounts and inventory using the QuickBooks software.

CHAPTER FOUR

BOOKKEEPING WITH QUICKBOOKS

Now that we have opened an account with QuickBooks and setup our first customers and vendors, it's time to get into the bookkeeping features QuickBooks has. In this chapter, you will learn how to create invoices and credit memos, learn the basic payroll service so that you can pay employees, connect your bank accounts, and track your inventory. By the time you're done this chapter, you will have a solid grasp on what goes into bookkeeping, and you'll be able to start managing all your bookkeeping needs through QuickBooks.

How to Create an Invoice

Invoices are a part of any business. They are like taxes that way. If you don't know what an invoice is, they are a document that details the products or services that your company has provided for the customer. They're one of the cornerstones of bookkeeping and they are required anytime a customer makes a purchase on credit. If your customer purchases your services but can pay at a later date, then you need to provide them with an invoice so that you can both keep track of the due date and the total cost. Using QuickBooks for invoices will let you see how much is owed to you on outstanding invoices, as well as how much is still left to be paid on invoices you've sent out.

This gives QuickBooks a big leg up when it comes to invoicing. If you were to invoice by hand, then you would always have to calculate how much is owed and how much you've received, and you would be responsible for updating the numbers every single time something changed. Using QuickBooks to handle your invoices will keep your numbers updated automatically so that all you have to do is glance at QuickBooks to see exactly where you are in terms of paid and owing numbers. But invoicing is made even easier than that, because QuickBooks lets you quickly create invoices, email them to clients, and even include a payment option within the digital invoice you send. All of this speed up how fast you get paid. So, let's create one.

The first step is to navigate to the creation form. There are two ways that you can do this. You can click on "invoice" off the side menu and then look for the new invoice button. The other way is to click on the button to open the create menu. This was the the plus sign button on the top right of the QuickBooks page.

From there, you can select "invoice" to go directly to the invoice creation form. While this is quicker, using the side menu to get there will first take you to a list of your invoices, and this can help prevent any accidents, such as creating a double of an invoice. It can be a good idea to build this double-check into how your business creates invoices, especially if there are multiple users under your QuickBooks account.

Once you have the create an invoice form open, you now have to fill out all the information about this particular invoice. You will see a drop menu to select which customer the invoice is for; if it is for a new customer, then at the top of the drop menu, you can click the add new button to have the customer creation form open so you can quickly add the new customer to QuickBooks without closing the invoice. When you select the customer, you will notice that their email address and billing address will auto-populate the form. You can edit either of these yourself from the invoice. Note that if you change the email address, it will update the corresponding customer's profile. However, if you update the billing address, it will not update the customer's profile. This can be a little annoying to remember but email addresses change far more often than billing addresses.

Also, in this section, you will see a couple boxes you can check. One is to allow payment via credit card. The other is to allow payment through bank transfer. Selecting either of these will include payment options within the invoice so that the customer can easily pay by clicking a button on the email they receive. This helps to speed up payment and make sure clients can see which payment options you accept without having to search for them on your website or contact you to ask.

The next section is the terms. The terms are how long the customer has to pay you. Terms auto populate depending on the terms you set in the customer profile, but you can change them from within here. Like changing an email address, doing this will change the terms set in their customer profile. QuickBooks will set the invoice's date to the day that you created it, but you can also change this if you need to. The date that payment is due will reflect the terms you have set for the invoice.

Once you finish the top section of the invoice, you then have to set which products or services the invoice covers. You select all the applicable services or products from the drop menu in this section. These are pulled from the services or products that you have created in QuickBooks. If you need to create a new product, then you will find the button to do so at the top of this drop menu. It will open the service or product creation form so that you can create whatever services you need without leaving the invoice. Each product or service will be followed by a description which is auto populated from the information you wrote in on the product or service creation form. If you write a custom description from within the invoice, it won't update the description that QuickBooks has saved. Next, you enter the quantity for each service or product on the invoice. How much it costs will be taken from the price that you have listed when you created the item. You can change this rate on the invoice without changing the saved listing.

You now have a complete invoice. On the bottom of the page, you should see a print preview button. Clicking this button will show you a preview of what the invoice will look like once it has been printed. This is a great time to double check that all of the information is correct. If you see a problem with the top half of the invoice, you know that one of your entry fields has a mistake in it. If there is something wrong with the services bought, like say you added two when they only bought one, you can go back and delete items by clicking the trash can symbol next to it. When you are satisfied with the invoice, it is time to send it to the customer.

You can always print out the invoice and give it to the customer in person, but chances are, your best bet is to use email. At the bottom of the invoice creation form is a save and close button with a drop menu arrow next to it. If you click this arrow, you will see an option to save and send. Click this to open a new preview of the invoice and send email form. The email address you are sending it to will auto populate from the customer profile. The subject line of the email will also auto populate, but this one will be generated by combining the invoice number and your company's name. The invoice number will automatically be generated by QuickBooks, so you don't have to worry about tracking them yourself. As for the body of the email, you will have to fill this in the same way you would any email you send. Click save to send queue, and the email will be sent off to the customer. The invoice will be a PDF attachment on the email that they receive.

How to Create a Credit Memo

Sometimes you make a mistake and an invoice with an extra item gets sent by accident. Or maybe there was a mistake made during the job, and you have to placate a customer by giving them some money back. Whatever the reason, it always sucks when it happens. At least QuickBooks makes it easy to take care of, so you can get back to focusing on the stuff that matters.

Open up the create menu from the plus sign button at the top of the page. Under the customers section you will see the credit memo button. Press that to pull up the credit memo creation form. This form is going to look a lot like the invoice form. First, select the customer that the credit memo is for. As you'll have noticed by now, QuickBooks is going to auto populate a lot of their information like their email address. Next, select the services or products that you are issuing the customer credit for. You can always change the price from the price that QuickBooks has listed. This is useful if you are giving half of their money back or a percentage of the purchase cost back to the customer.

The subtotal of the credit memo will show underneath the list of products or services that you have input. This is the total amount of credit that you will be giving the customer, not the total cost or charge. Before you send the credit memo, you can add a message to be displayed on the credit memo, such as an explanation of what the credit is for or a thank you letter. You can also add a memo. The memo is used for within your QuickBooks account so that you never forget the purpose of the credit memo. This memo is purely internal, so the customer won't be able to see anything you write here.

When you have double-checked the credit memo and approve of everything, then it is time to save the memo. Like with invoices, you can save and send credit memos out at the same time by selecting the save and send option from the drop menu by the save button. The credit memo will be sent off to the customer's email address, and the financial information will be calculated automatically in QuickBooks.

Introduction to Payroll

Payroll is a major component of running any business. Your employees have to get paid after all. But despite the fact that every business with employees have to deal with payroll, it is still one of the most annoying and complicated parts of any business. QuickBooks will help to make this easier. But first, let's learn a little more about payroll.

Payroll simply refers to the total amount of money that your company pays to its employees. When we talk about payroll in relation to QuickBooks, we're actually speaking on the act of paying the employees and the paperwork involved therein. Dealing with payroll means handling insurance premiums, taxes, and retirement plan contributions, which makes calculating an employee's pay a complicated process.

There are four major parts of payroll. First, you have gross wages. This number is simply how much the employee makes before anything is deducted from their pay. Say an employee makes $10 an hour and worked for ten hours. They would have $100 of gross wages, but this number is before taxes or any other deductions, so it is off from the final number. If your company provides health insurance and other benefits such as a retirement plan, then there is likely going to be a deduction there that has to be calculated. You also must deduct social security and medicare payments from the gross wages, and some states will have other governmental deductions that have to be calculated. The final part is taxes, which means that your company holds the income taxes from the payroll. After all of this is deducted from the gross pay, the amount left over that the employee actually gets is called the net pay.

The reason that payroll is one of the most tedious parts of running a business is because it's up to you, the company, to figure out the federal and state income taxes that need to be deducted from each pay period. In order to do this, you need to submit tax withholding reports whenever you send payments. To do this, you need to first have each of your employees fill out a form W-4 from the IRS so that you can compute withholding allowances. After allowances are calculated, you then have to calculate federal income taxes by using IRS Publication 15. The federal taxes your company is withholding typically gets paid to the government at the same time that the social security and medicare deductions are paid, which can be reported with form 941 from the IRS. Federal tax rates will be in the form of a percentage with a maximum that can be deducted each year. This percentage is subtracted from your employees each and every time they are paid. Your company also matches the amount that is deducted from social security and medicare taxes. If the employee has $10 deducted from their paycheck, then the company also contributes $10 to make the total payment to the government $20.

Because there is so much involved in it, running payroll can be a pain, and it is easy to miss something.

Each employee needs to fill out paperwork about health insurance if they want to participate, though they can also opt out. If you have a retirement plan, then you have to get that paperwork from the employees, which again, they can opt out of if they so choose. Every worker has to fill out a form W-4 from the IRS, and this is one they can't opt out of legally. If you've gotten all the forms back, it is still easy to miss something. Let's take a look at the step-by-step process for payroll, and then we'll take a look at how QuickBooks helps to make it that much easier.

First thing's first, you have to figure out the gross pay for the employee you are making these calculations for. Once you have that number, you can then work out all the deductions and remove this much from the employee's pay to end up at their net pay. Paying your employee is perhaps the next most important step. You then forward the deducted money to the insurance companies, send it off for the retirement plan or wherever that particular employee has agreed to. Next, you have to submit the taxes that you deducted to the proper taxing authorities. Anywhere along this line you may run into paperwork from insurance companies, retirement companies, or the taxing authorities, and this may slow up the whole process with a lot of red tape. This is particularly true when first setting up employees, though it typically runs much smoother once they have settled into the system.

If you're hiring freelancers rather than employees, you will have a much easier time as you simply pay them their gross pay and let them deduct their own taxes and benefits. But if you want to make payroll for employees easier, then it's time to start using QuickBooks as your payroll application.

Adding Employees and Pay Schedules

When it takes so much work to figure out paying your employees, it's easy to understand why someone would want to pick up the QuickBooks add-on to make it run a lot smoother. If you have purchased the payroll add-on then you can get to paying your employees much faster and easier by following these steps.

First, we must get all our payment information into QuickBooks. To do this, navigate to the employee's page from the sidebar menu. If you haven't set up any employees yet, don't worry that's okay. What you want to do is find the blue button that says "get started with payroll." This will trigger a popup with some questions that QuickBooks needs you to answer beforehand. They'll want to know if you have paid any W-2 employees yet this year. W-2 just means that they are a regular employee rather than a freelancer. The next question is to see if you have had your employees fill out a W-4 form yet. As we saw above, you are legally required to have your employees fill out a W-4, so if you have employees already, then you most certainly should have these forms. If you haven't had them filled out yet, QuickBooks includes a link to them alongside this question.

With these initial questions out of the way, it is now time to begin adding your employees to QuickBooks. Each employee that you have and pay should be added to QuickBooks. You will notice that the employee page looks as empty as the customers page did when we first began. As you add employees to QuickBooks, you will be able to find them here and see how many hours they've worked and how much they have earned through your company. To add your employees, click on the add employee button which should be to the bottom left of the employee list (which is currently empty).

The employee creation form will also look similar to the customer creation form, though there are some important key differences. Entering the employee's name is straight forward enough, and once that is out of the way, you then have to enter payment information. Click on the button labelled "enter W-4 form" to open up a new section to fill out. Here, you will need to provide the address, social security number, and marital status of the employee you are adding to QuickBooks. Using the W-4 form that you had them fill out, you can enter the numbers required for the allowances you are claiming and any additional amount you want to withhold from each paycheck. Once you have all this information filled in, then you can click the done button. This will close the W-4 input section of the employee creation form.

Next, it's time to enter the payment schedule that the employee will run on. Chances are good that this will be the same as everyone else in the company, but if you have employees with unique payment schedules, you can set them apart from each other during this step. Click enter a pay schedule to open up the pay schedule form. From the drop-down box, select how often that employee gets paid: weekly, bi-weekly, twice a month or once a month. You'll notice as you start to select options on the left, that the pay schedule on the right matches your selections to show you when the next four pay periods would occur. After you select how often you want to pay, enter the date of the next payday and when the hours for that payday reset. Using the project schedule, double-check everything and fine tune it. Once you are satisfied, you can name the pay schedule. If you are using the same pay schedule for all or most of your employees, then you will want to check the box on the bottom left to automatically give this pay schedule to any new employees you add to QuickBooks.

With the schedule out of the way, it is onto step three, and this one is easy. Set out the employee's pay. Just put in their rate, whether it is hourly or salary, and that's done. Unless you pay overtime, sick pay, vacation pay or anything like that. If this is the case, then you will need to click the add additional pay types button. This opens up a menu with some boxes to check. These let you add overtime, double overtime, sick, vacation, holiday, bonus and commission payment options. You can easily check these to include these common additional payment forms. If you happen to have some kind of payment form that is not included here, then you can find a second menu of options from here as well.

Once you fill out section three, you should notice the check on the right side of the screen is starting to fill out and look like a real financial document. This is because now that you are getting all their information in, QuickBooks can actually begin doing the background calculations required for the employee's payroll. QuickBooks makes it really easy to do payroll because it is handling these complicated calculations so you have more time to focus on any issues at hand.

If your employee has any deductions listed on their W-4 form then you will want to click the pencil button on section four to add those in. If they don't, which is the most common response, then you can just click no and head to section five. Here, you get to decide how you pay the employee. Like section four, you'll want to click the edit button. From the drop-down menu, select if you would rather use a paper check, direct deposit, direct deposit to two accounts, or direct deposit with the balance as a check.

With that, you have created your first employee. In all likelihood, you will be doing this a few times to get all your employees into QuickBooks before you run a payroll. You'll also want to wait until your employees have gotten a few hours into the books. Let's pretend that it has been a week, and now you want to pay the employee you just added. To do that, we have to run the payroll.

Using the Basic Payroll Service

It's time to pay your employees. If you aren't already on the employee page then go there now using the sidebar menu. Where you originally clicked the get started with payroll button to begin entering your employees and setting up the pay schedule, you will now see a button to run payroll. Clicking this will bring up the payroll service you need.

The payroll service appears as a list of your employees. To the top left, you set which bank account the money will be coming out of. We'll get your bank accounts added to QuickBooks in the next step. To the right is the information regarding which pay period this particular payroll is covering. Below these options are the employees. You'll notice that you enter in how many hours they worked here. If you checked any additional payment options when you were creating your employees, like overtime or vacation pay, then you can put in those hours separately from their regular pay hours. Once you have all the hours in place, click the preview payroll button on the bottom right of the screen.

On the preview page you will see the total pay, the taxes, and the net pay for every employee. You will also be shown how many checks are required (typically there is only one per employee). The graph that QuickBooks uses and the numbers they show make it very easy for employers to see exactly how much they are paying to employees every payroll. When you are satisfied that everything is correct, then it is time to submit the payroll. You can print the pay stubs from this final window. You can print paychecks from QuickBooks, too, if you don't use direct deposit. Remember to give each employee's pay a check number. This is important for your bookkeeping and so that QuickBooks can do all of its necessary calculations.

That's it! QuickBooks makes it super easy to run payroll and make sure that all of your employees are getting their proper pay. By using QuickBooks' basic payroll, you are able to cut out basically all of the math that you would have had to do, and instead, let the QuickBooks application take care of it for you. This helps to cut down on human errors that crop up when doing lots of math by hand.

But if you want to pay your employees, then you need to have an account from which to pay them. For that, we need to add our banking information.

Connecting Your Bank Accounts to QuickBooks

Getting your bank accounts into QuickBooks is an easy process, though it will take a little bit of time to sort transactions initially. To get started connecting your bank, you don't even need to leave the QuickBooks dashboard. To the right side, you will see the bank accounts header, beneath which should be a button to connect an account. Click this to open up a new window.

From here, you will need to select your bank. Some of the most popular banks are listed so that all you have to do is click on their names, but if you don't see yours here, you can search for your bank or enter your bank's URL in the search bar at the top. When you have found your bank, you need to then log in using the QuickBooks login popup. Entering your bank through QuickBooks will give your QuickBooks permission to access balances and transactions from your account. Once you have connected to your bank, you need to choose which accounts QuickBooks will have permission to see. Select whichever account you use for your business transactions. You will have to tell QuickBooks what kind of account it is, either checking, savings, credit card, money market, or trust. Once you have selected the type, click the connect button to your left.

Connecting your account will have QuickBooks download any transactions on the account from the last 90 days. Head to the bank and credit cards page by first opening the transactions tab on the side menu and then clicking on banking. You should see a list of all the transactions that QuickBooks has pulled into its files. If you added multiple accounts, you will notice that on the top of this page, you can click on checking, savings, credit card, or whatever combination of accounts you brought into QuickBooks. Clicking on one of these will bring up the transactions associated with that account so that you always know what account you are sorting at any given time.

You'll notice that each transaction includes the date on which it occurred, a box to describe what it was, a payee, category, and then financial information covering whether money went into or out of the account. QuickBooks tries its best to automatically assign categories to all transactions. It is important to look over these transactions and confirm that they are categorized properly. If you notice something is sorted wrong, then it's time to edit the transaction.

Click on the transaction to expand it into the transaction editor. Here, you have a bunch of options to customize the transaction. You can split it into two transactions if you want, such as if you have receipts and want to separate items in the QuickBooks application. You can add GST or HST to the records. There is an option to leave a memo for company use. Most importantly, you can change the transaction category or the payee. In the drop-down for categories, you will see a bunch of different categories. These are used by QuickBooks to generate reports, so it is important to sort your transactions into their proper categories. You can also change the payee, which is a great way to personalize and get some specific information into the transaction. If a payee is not in your QuickBooks application yet, then you can click the drop-down menu to find the add new button at the top. This lets you enter a payee. Fill out their name and the type of payee they are, like supplier, and hit save. You can always add more details if you need to, but QuickBooks makes it easy to enter new payees to help you sort your books.

If QuickBooks is correct in categorizing a bunch of your payments, then you can select them together by holding down the shift key and selecting the top check box. Click the check box at the bottom of the list to select everything in between your two points. You can unselect anything you don't want to batch edit. With this many selected, you will see a batch actions button at the top of the list which will allow you to approve all the selected transactions in only a couple of clicks.

You can check all of the transactions that you have approved by filtering your transaction list by those within QuickBooks. Underneath where you have selected which account you want to look at, you will notice three tabs. These are new transactions in QuickBooks and excluded transactions. When transactions are first pulled into QuickBooks, they show up under the new transaction tab. You have to approve them from here. Once you have approved a transaction, it moves into QuickBooks proper. To see these transactions, you have to switch to the QuickBooks tab. If you make a mistake on any transaction, then you can always click on the transaction and hit the undo button on the right most column. This will move it back to the new transaction section, and you can re-sort or edit it however it requires.

That's all there is to setting up your bank accounts within QuickBooks. Doing this gives QuickBooks all the numbers it needs to give you a live update of your accounts. This information will be used in tons of reports, and you see how much you have every time you pay your employees. By adding your banks to QuickBooks, you start to tap into the full power of the QuickBooks system.

Setting Up Products and Keeping Track of Inventory

It's important to keep track of your inventory and know how much it costs you to make or purchase the items that you're selling, how much you are making off each one, and how many you have in stock at any given time. If you don't know how much stock you have, you can easily oversell and disappoint customers. By keeping track of inventory, you are able to see which items are hot movers so that you can make sure to order more before you run out. This also helps you to see how much you are making off each product, which helps you to fine-tune your offerings based on what will actually make money.

To step up inventory tracking in QuickBooks, first click on the gear icon from the top menu and open the account and settings window. From the left menu, select the option that says sales. Click the pencil icon to edit this page and look for the check box that tracks inventory quantity on hand. This option turns on the tracking features. You have to go into the settings and change this first because it is defaulted as off when you first sign up for QuickBooks.

Once you have saved your new settings, head over to the products page. Like with customers and vendors, you will at first find an empty page. You have to click the new button and make your first products. You can create services, non-inventory products, or bundle up services and products you already have created. Select the top option, inventory, to continue exploring inventory tracking. This will trigger the product creation form, with added sections to fill out for tracking purposes.

Enter the name of the product and upload a picture of the product if you have one. You must have a name, but the picture is an optional field. Also optional is the SKU. The SKU is a unique number with which to identify the product. It can be useful to give products SKUs for bookkeeping purposes, but it is not a requirement. Use the category drop-down menu to help with the sorting of your products and services.

Now let's get into the inventory tracking additions. Initial quantity on hand is a required field, and here is where you tell QuickBooks how many of the product you have stocked currently. After you create a product, you won't be able to change the number in stock without entering an inventory adjustment, so make sure that you double-check this initial quantity before approving the product. The as of date is also a requirement and it tells QuickBooks the date at which to begin tracking the quantity of the product. The reorder point is not a requirement but is a useful feature. By selecting the minimum amount of the product that you want to have on hand, QuickBooks will notify you upon reaching that quantity so that you can order more from your vendors or manufacturers. The inventory asset account is another required field. This is automatically filled out by QuickBooks to link to your inventory asset account from the chart of accounts. If you want to change the account which this product is associated with, then you just have to enter the preferred account here.

Next, you want to enter the sales information. This field is a description of the product that appears on invoices and sales receipts. This is a great place to put a short description of the product so that it is automatically populated in later invoices and you don't have to worry about filling out the information each and every time you sell this product. The sales price/rate field is where you put how much you sell the product for. You can always leave it blank if you don't have a set price. The income account section is another requirement. Here you will set the account used for tracking income from any sales of the product. Like the inventory asset account setting, this will be auto populated but you can always set it manually. The purchasing information section is only used for when you want to create purchase orders. You can enter a description as you'd want to see it listed on any purchase orders. You can always leave this blank. The cost field is how much you pay for the product. You don't have to fill it out, but this helps QuickBooks calculate how much you are making or losing on the products that you sell. Finally, the expense account field is another one that links to the chart of accounts, and you can change it as you need to. Double-check the information you've entered and then save the product when you are satisfied.

Now that you actually have a product and some inventory that QuickBooks is tracking, it's time to figure out how to get reports on your inventory. Head over to the reports page by using the sidebar menu. On the reports page, look for the all reports tab and click it when you find it. Here you will find a list of the different reports you can run. Look for the product/service list heading. Once you find that, you will see a blue button to run it. Click that to generate a report on your inventory. It will tell you how much you have on hand, how much you can expect to make off the item and how much it cost you to acquire. If you sell any items, come back and run it again to see that QuickBooks automatically updates the information based on the transactions and invoices you are sending. Don't forget, you'll also get a notification when you are starting to run low on inventory, so you'll never miss restocking again.

Chapter Summary

- QuickBooks makes invoicing even easier by giving you options to send them directly from QuickBooks, keep track of which have or haven't been paid, and even offer options for customers to pay directly from the invoice.
- To create an invoice, you need to open the invoice creation form which can be found easily through the create menu at the top of the screen.
- Use the drop menus of the invoice creation form to pick the customer it is for and set the products or services that the customer has purchased on that particular invoice.
- From the invoice creation screen, if you change the customer's email then it will save the new email address to their corresponding customer entry in QuickBooks.
- Select the check boxes at the top of the invoice creation form to allow customers to pay you directly through the invoice.
- At the bottom of the invoice creation form will be a save button. You can use the drop arrow next to this button to select the save and send option which allows you to email the invoice to the customer directly through QuickBooks.

- If you overcharge a customer or they want a return, you need to issue them a credit memo. This is very similar to the invoice creation process.
- Use the quick create button and select the credit memo button. Select the customer the credit memo is for and then select the services or products that you are crediting them. This looks almost exactly like an invoice except that you are offering credit rather than receiving income, and so the amount listed represents an expense.
- Payroll is the process you run in order to pay your employees. It is overly complicated and a real pain to do by hand. That's why QuickBooks' basic payroll add-on exists.
- Payroll sees the gross wages that employees make get deducted for taxes and any other deductions they may have in order to figure out their net pay.
- Every employee must fill out an IRS W-4 form, both legally and so you can make use of QuickBooks' payroll features.
- In order to pay employees, you must first have employees and set up the payroll features. You do this by clicking the get started with payroll button on the employee's page.
- QuickBooks will ask you some questions about your payment history and then bring you into the employee creation form. Here,

you add all the information about your employees including how much they make and the information from their W-4 forms. By the time you finish, QuickBooks will have everything it needs to begin paying your staff.

- When creating your first employee, you will be asked to create their pay schedule. This can be saved with the click of a button to have QuickBooks automatically add new employees to the same schedule.
- Once you have employees created, you can run the payroll. Where you clicked the get started button will now be a button to run payroll.
- Add each employee's hours worked for that pay period to have QuickBooks calculate their earnings and deductions for you. You can even print off pay stubs or checks from here if you need to.
- Connecting your bank account to QuickBooks lets you keep track of all your transactions to easily keep up with your bookkeeping needs.
- On the QuickBooks dashboard, select the connect an account option under banks. Find the bank you use, and log in to select which accounts to connect with QuickBooks.
- The last 90 days of transactions will be pulled into QuickBooks for any account you select.

Head over to the transactions page to see the new entries.

- Approve, edit, or deny transactions as you see fit. Those you approve will be brought into QuickBooks and will factor into the financial information they are using in calculating your accounts.
- To track inventory in QuickBooks, you first have to click on the options menu and navigate to the sales settings. Here, you'll find a check box to have QuickBooks track your inventory. Select it and save.
- When you create a new product, you will have to select the inventory option so that QuickBooks knows to track your new item. When creating an inventory product, you must also answer some questions about how much is in stock currently.

In the next chapter, you will learn how to use QuickBooks for your accounting needs. We'll cover preparing financial statements, how we get use the reporting features, and how we can use QuickBooks to help us with budgeting.

CHAPTER FIVE

ACCOUNTING WITH QUICKBOOKS

Now that we have gone through the motions of transitioning our bookkeeping into QuickBooks, we are now able to use it for our accounting needs. The information and steps we walked through in the previous chapter, our bookkeeping, gives us the data that is required to make use of the accounting options of this chapter. This is why bookkeeping and accounting are so tightly connected.

In this chapter, we'll learn how to prepare a profit and loss statement and begin customizing your own reports, how to manage budgets with QuickBooks, and how to outsource to an accountant or bookkeeper.

How to Prepare Financial Statements

Financial statements are used to help you understand how your company is doing based directly on the data gathered by operating. One of the most important of the financial statements is the profit and loss statement. This statement compares your income and your expenses to show you exactly where your bottom line is. You run profit and loss statements to cover a few days or even whole quarters of the year, but you should be running one at least once a month in order to stay up to date with your finances.

Head over to the reports page from the sidebar menu. This will take you to the recommend reports page. The first option should be the profit and loss report. If it isn't, you can always find the report under the all reports option. As you begin to use more reports, you'll be able to find the ones that you use most under the frequently run tab. For now, let's click on the blue run button next to the profit and loss report.

The first time you run a report, QuickBooks will bring up the report basis box. Here, you can enter cash basis or accrual basis. Cash basis means that you count income and expenses only when you actually receive or pay money. Accrual basis means that you count income or expenses as soon as you receive a bill or send an invoice. A lot of companies use cash rather than accrual because it is easier and also reflects the money that is currently in the account at any time rather than the money that may or may not be in, depending on how long it takes those invoices to be paid.

The next screen lets you change the report filters. You can print, email, or export the report. You can also customize the report, which we'll look at doing in the next section. Most important here is the fact that you have to set the transaction date for the report. This is the time period which the report will cover. Click the run report button and take a look at your profit and loss statement.

The profit and loss report that you created has four key sections. The first is your income. This covers how much money you made for the period of time the report covered. Section two is the cost of producing your products. Section three shows the expenses that you've had to cover during the time period. The final section is the net income section. This calculates how much money you actually gained or lost by calculating the other three sections for you.

With that, you have made a financial statement. It was pretty easy because we just ran the report on its own. It should look pretty boring at this point. Let's personalize our reports a little going forward so that people know they are for our company.

Customizing Reports

Creating reports is super easy, as you saw with the profit and loss report, but they are definitely boring to look at. QuickBooks makes it easy to personalize your reports to give them some flair and personality. It also makes it easier for sorting purposes. If your reports have your logo and information on them, then it's harder to confuse them with all the other paperwork that comes with running a business.

Head over to the reports page by using the sidebar menu and pick a report. Since it is the first one that pops up, and you just saw how it looks if you don't customize it, select the profit and loss report. Look for the customize button on the report filters page. If you have run a profit and loss report before, then you won't have to worry about selecting between a cash or accrual basis.

Clicking the customize button will open a popup with the many options available for you to tinker with. You will see tabs for general customization, row/column, filter, and header/foot customization as well. In the general customization, you can change the report period, the reporting basis, and the number format of your report. Under the rows/columns tab, you can play around with how the information is displayed on the final report. Filter allows you to designate parts of your finances that you want withheld from the report you are customizing. The header/footer section is where you can add in things like your company's logo and name, the report title and period, the date and time it was prepared, and what accounting basis it is using. In order to get the company name or logo, you must go to your account settings and add these details there. QuickBooks then uses that information to fill out the header and add the logo when you select them here. Save your customizations when you're satisfied. You can add this custom report to a group, such as management reports, to easily access your customized report anytime you want to run it again. Find it under the table called "my custom reports" on the reports page.

You can customize any of the reports within QuickBooks, whether it is a profit and loss report or a sales report. Select the reports you are likely to use most often, customize them, and then save them for easy access. Getting all the customizations out of the way first will make sure that your reports always look the same and have your company's stamp for easy identification.

Budgeting with QuickBooks

QuickBooks Online Plus and QuickBooks Online Advanced both include a budgeting feature so that you can use the data within your QuickBooks application to keep on top of your expenses and make sure that every dollar is heading to the right place. Since the best time to make a new budget is at the start of the year, we should first set up when our fiscal year begins.

To set the beginning of your fiscal year, first click on the gear button at the top of the screen and enter the account settings. Select advanced from the right-hand menu and look for the accounting section. You'll find a date field that lets you select the first month of the fiscal year. Set it to whenever you plan to begin your fiscal year by clicking the pencil icon next to the field. Save the setting and exit back to the dashboard.

Now let's get to building that budget. Click on the gear button again and this time select the budgeting option that you'll see under the tool's header, then look for the add budget button. In here, you'll have to enter the budget's name and select the fiscal year that the budget covers. You can use the drop menu under interval to select whether you want to create a monthly budget, a quarterly budget or a yearly budget. Under prefill data, you can tell QuickBooks to automatically grab data from the current or the previous fiscal year when making the budget. Under the subdivide option, you select whether you want QuickBooks to split up the budget depending on class, customer, or location and select which categories you want to include in the budget. Both this subdivision and the prefill data sections are optional settings to help you craft a budget around your specific needs. Hit next to head to the following step.

If you did not prefill any data in the previous step, then you will enter data into the table provided. Enter the amounts that are necessary keeping in mind that QuickBooks does not round to the nearest dollar so include cents using a decimal point. As you are setting your budget on the various accounts that you have, you may notice that some accounts seem to be missing.

If you encounter this problem, click the gear icon above the total column and make sure that the hide blank rows option is not selected. Once you have the numbers of your budget in place, save it and exit out.

Once you have a budget created, you can now generate a budget overview and the budget versus actuals report. The budget overview report gives you a quick summary of your budget, while the budget versus actuals report gives you an overview of how much you have budgeted compared to the actual income and expenses accrued. Click the gear button at the top, and under tools find the budgeting option again. Find the budget you have created and from the drop menu in the action's column, you will find the run budget overview report and run budget vs. actuals report buttons. Click either of these to generate a budget report which you can then email, print or save. You can also export the budget to Excel or PDF formats if need be. If you need to edit the budget, you can also do so by using the drop menu from the action column. Select edit this time to change the budget name or dollar amounts as need be. Save and close the budget when you have made the necessary changes.

You may find yourself wanting to play around with your budget and try out some new ideas about where money should go. Instead of doing this on a budget that is in place currently, you can instead duplicate that budget. Duplicating a budget may also be used to take last year's budget and put it into place for the coming fiscal year. Whatever the reason, duplicating a budget is easy in QuickBooks. Under the action category, click on copy. This will open a copy budget popup from which you enter the duplicated budget's name and you can change the fiscal year as you need to. Hit create budget. The budget in front of you now should be a duplicate of the budget you copied, only with a different year or name as you have chosen. You can now play around with this budget to see if there are better ways of allocating your money, safe in the knowledge that you have a copy of the budget that hasn't been altered in any way.

When you are done with your duplicated budget, or if you accidentally created a budget that you don't need, then you can easily delete it by selecting the delete action from the drop menu you have been using to edit and generate budget reports. Remember that once you delete a budget, you can't undo the action. If you delete a budget that you still needed, you will have to recreate the budget and enter all the information again by hand.

Collaborating with an Accountant or Bookkeeper

Even with all the tools that QuickBooks offers, it can be really challenging to keep up with your books and figure out your bottom line if numbers and finances give you a headache. Sometimes it is best to reach out to a professional accountant or bookkeeper to help you. If you use an outside agent like a tax professional or the like, then you want to give them access to your QuickBooks so that they can do their jobs. QuickBooks makes it easy to add multiple users so you can leave the numbers to the pros.

To add users to your QuickBooks, you need to select the gear icon at the top and look for the option that says "manage users." From here you can add users, but since we're adding an accountant or a bookkeeper, let's click on the accountant's tab at the top. This pops up an invite box to send an email to your accountant. Enter their email address and click invite, and they will be able to come onto your QuickBooks. They will follow a link from their email to sign in to your QuickBooks account. They will make their own user ID. As soon as they open up your QuickBooks, you will be able to see that their status on the user's page becomes active.

Your accountant will be given company administrator privileges. This means that the accountant will be able to access all of the QuickBooks data and has the ability to close the books on past periods. You can always create a new user through the traditional user creation form to create standard users. Standard users allow you to set who can see specific areas of QuickBooks and could be useful for tax professionals. However, accountant user profiles are best created in the accountant section so they can have access to everything they need.

Chapter Summary

- QuickBooks makes it easy to generate financial statements using the reports feature.
- The first time you run a report, it will ask you to set the basis as either cash or accrual. This means your data will either run off the cash you have actually had move through your accounts or by the money you are owed through invoices and the like.
- To prepare a statement, click on the reports section and search for the report you want to run. You can find the available reports under the all reports section. As you use more reports, you will find your most used under the frequently run section.
- You can print, email or export the reports you generate in QuickBooks for easy distribution.
- Customizing your reports is easy and lets you add your business's personal flair to your documents.
- Select customize report when creating your report and use these options to design reports to your specifications. You can save customizations through here.
- Saved customizations appear under the custom reports tab.

- QuickBooks can help you to set a budget. First, head to the account settings page and set the beginning of your fiscal year under the accounting tab.
- Select budgeting under the tools header to pull up the budgeting creation form from which you enter your budgeted amounts.
- Once you have created a budget, you can generate budget overviews and budget vs. actuals reports. It can be valuable to run one of both to see how they compare to each other.
- Collaborating with an accountant or a bookkeeper is a great way to ensure that all of your financial data is handled properly.
- To bring your accountant into QuickBooks, head to the add user section and add your financial professional under the accountant tab.
- You can also add any users who work for your company from the add user section, but use the first section that opens and not the accountant section.
- The accountant section grants high level permissions to the user you create, whereas the general create users section creates users whose permissions you can limit.

In the next chapter, you will learn a ton of helpful tips and tricks to ensure that your experience with QuickBooks is as smooth as possible.

CHAPTER SIX

HELPFUL TIPS

By this point, you should have a solid grasp on the QuickBooks accounting and bookkeeping system. From creating an account to paying your employees and collaborating with an accountant, you now have the tools to use QuickBooks as your accounting system for your own business. In order to make sure you get off to as smooth of a start as possible, this chapter will be looking at how to keep your financial information safe, how to connect apps to get even more functionality out of the QuickBooks platform, and we'll look at some common mistakes people make with QuickBooks. With all this information, you will have what you need to use QuickBooks like a pro.

Connecting Third Party Apps to Your QuickBooks Account

There are a ton of third-party apps available for you to connect to your QuickBooks and individualize your experience. There is nowhere near enough room in this book to tackle them all considering there are more than 270 of them. Thankfully, installing apps is far easier and a more uniform experience than using them.

You can find apps for QuickBooks by heading over the apps page of QuickBooks Online. Interestingly, a Google search will also take you to Intuit's app store. Using an internet browser to checkout the apps allows users to see what options are available before they even purchase a QuickBooks plan. Clicking on apps, you can find a learn more button to figure out if they are any good for your purposes. You can read about the app, check out the reviews and pricing, and find any contact information you might need in the support section. The support section often includes frequently asked questions as well.

Once you have settled on an app that you wish to connect, look for the get app now button. Click that button and then authorize the app by clicking on authorize in the bottom right corner of the popup. Authorizing the app allows it to connect to your QuickBooks data and for QuickBooks to connect to the app. Once authorized, the app will be installed to your QuickBooks account and you are ready to use it as you like.

How to Keep Your Data Secure

When it comes to the list of data that you want to keep secure, financial data is probably the top kind. Reports of stolen credit cards are among the media's favorite stories of hacking scares. QuickBooks cares about your privacy and security and so they make sure that your data is protected at all times. But beyond hacking, what if something were to happen to your data and you lost it? This would set you back and mean a lot of man-hours spent re-logging old numbers. QuickBooks makes sure to keep your data not just protected against hackers, but it also has tools to prevent it from becoming lost.

One of the ways that QuickBooks keeps your data safe is by backing it up regularly. Whenever your data is updated, it is stored on mirrored disks. This means that it is stored on multiple hard drives rather than just one. If one of the hard drives fails, your data is still secure on the other hard drive. In fact, you wouldn't even know that the hard drive had failed because you would still have access to everything at all times. Now, I know what you're thinking, what if both hard drives get damaged? QuickBooks thought of that too. That's why they periodically make a copy of the data into yet another hard drive. Each night, the data is backed up to tape and moved to a secure location. QuickBooks understands how important your financial information is, so they don't take risks when it comes to backing it up.

QuickBooks also uses a powerful firewall to help protect your data. This makes it hard for hackers to break in and steal your data. QuickBooks makes use of SSL technology, which is the same tech that online credit card transactions use to keep your numbers safe. You can lose your credit card information by making purchases on unprotected sites. With QuickBooks Online, you are using their site which has been secured. This means there is less risk using QuickBooks than there is using your credit card online. Another issue is viruses. Many people's computers have viruses from exploring sketchy websites while unprotected. This exposes the data on their computer to potential threats. However, QuickBooks Online stores your data on their servers. These servers are well-protected by firewall and antivirus protection. This means that using QuickBooks Online will offer you far more protection than the average user's computer would.

Another way that QuickBooks protects your data is by the password and ID system. We had to set up a new ID when we brought our accountant into QuickBooks. You'll remember that it showed us when he was logged in and when he was offline. This is another security measure to help protect your data. Every person that uses your QuickBooks has to have a unique ID and password. When they are logged on, they are tracked. If you are having problems or noticing weird activity, QuickBooks support will be able to check these logs of who was on and when. This means that they can track who was doing what when. This helps you to identify mistakes or catch which IDs have been compromised if you are dealing with a security issue.

While those are QuickBooks' core ways of keeping your data safe, there are also steps that you should be taking to ensure your data remains uncompromised. One of the abilities you have as the owner of the QuickBooks account is to restrict access for your users. Click on the gear button and head to users and passwords. You can add users from here or edit users. Editing users will give you the option to restrict their access based on which sections you approve them for. This helps to prevent users from editing or seeing data that is irrelevant to their duties.

Make sure that you have an antivirus and firewall installed on any computers which you use for work. Make sure to update these as new updates become available. You should also be keeping your operating system and internet browsers up to date with the latest updates. These updates patch holes in the defences of applications, so to have the most protection possible you, should be working with the newest versions. Make sure that work computers aren't used for browsing the web leisurely. Many websites across the net are compromised and lowering the risk of exposure ensures better protection for your data. Never use work computers on unsecured networks such as the free wifi at the coffee shop. Excessive browsing and unsecured networks risk exposing your data to unnecessary risks. QuickBooks works hard to keep your data secure, but you have to meet them halfway.

Mistakes to Avoid

When it comes to using QuickBooks, mistakes can actually be quite devastating. Since we are dealing with financial information within QuickBooks, any mistakes we make put our financial statements and our bookkeeping at risk. This means that mistakes can really lead to chaos, as our financial information no longer seems to make sense or it reflects different numbers from reality. To make sure that you don't commit the same common mistakes that other QuickBooks users have found themselves making, let's take a look at some of the most frequent mistakes that pop up when people use QuickBooks. If you find yourself guilty of a few of these yourself, remember, there is no better time to fix them then now.

Mistake: Failing to Reconcile Your Bank Accounts

When you first connect your bank account with QuickBooks, you have to go through and sort the transactions into categories (like we saw in chapter four). Doing this is the first step to connecting your bank account and the most important. However, mistakes can make it through this sorting process. For example, you may have the same transaction listed twice or the transaction may have ended up in the wrong account. If when you go to run a financial report, you find that your balance is way off (like, so far off that it makes no sense), this means you probably have some reconciling to do.

Reconciling your bank accounts is the process of matching the transactions you pulled into QuickBooks with the transactions from your bank account itself. You do this to ensure that QuickBooks hasn't made a mistake while importing data from your bank. You should reconcile your accounts on a regular schedule, just to be safe. Don't worry though, QuickBooks offers tools to help make reconciling easier.

First, go and grab your bank statements relating to the account that you are reconciling. These you'll find through your online banking or by stopping at a physical bank. Either way, you will be the one to find these rather than QuickBooks.

Now, click on the gear icon on the top menu and look for the reconcile option under the tools heading. Clicking reconcile will open a new page. First, you must select the account which you want to reconcile. For now, select checking and hit the reconcile now button. The start reconciling popup requires that you enter in the bank statement's end date and the ending balance. Once you have entered the date and balance, click OK.

QuickBooks will then open the reconciling tool. You will see all the different transactions laid out before you. With your bank statement at hand, match each transaction from QuickBooks with its corresponding transaction from your statement. When a transaction in QuickBooks matches with a transaction on the bank statement, go ahead and click the check mark to the far left of the transaction. Remember, you only need to click on that small check box. If you click on the transaction itself, this will open another window and it may be confusing to get back to the reconciling page.

After you have reconciled all the transactions, you can tell it has been done properly based on the bottom of the page. You will see a beginning balance, statement ending balance, cleared balance, and difference row on the bottom of the screen. When you have properly cleared all the transactions, you will see that the difference at the very bottom will show as $0. If you are doing your banking information by hand, then there is a higher chance that there is an issue here. Bank service charges, checks that haven't yet cleared and transactions which you forgot to log into QuickBooks are some of the most common causes of differences between your bank statement and your QuickBooks data. If you are showing a difference value above zero, you will have to examine what the difference is and use your detective skills to figure out where it is coming from.

If your difference value is at $0, click the finish now button. You can now view that reconciliation as a report. Under the reconcile option from the top gear menu, you will be brought to the page you first began reconciling from. However, now you will see your reconciliation report listed. Clicking that report lets you open it. Once open, you can print it out and attach it to your bank statement. This will help out your accountant, and it will help you out at tax time.

Reconciling your account is a way to make sure that QuickBooks is running with the proper information. Because it can catch mistakes that mess up your accounts, it is best to reconcile on a regular schedule, such as once a month. Remember, too, that you should also be reconciling your credit card accounts and savings accounts. Basically, any account that you have connected to QuickBooks should be reconciled monthly.

Mistake: Keeping Your Chart of Accounts Messy

When you first signed up for QuickBooks, it went ahead and automatically generated some accounts for your chart of accounts. While these auto-generated accounts make up the bulk of what a company typically needs, you may want to go in and add accounts of your own. However, adding accounts and keeping accounts that you don't need can be a real pain later on. The more accounts you have, the more likely it is for an error to occur. Basically, the more options you have to sort your data into, the more likely it is that you will accidently sort your data wrong. There are a few steps you can take to clean up your chart of accounts and help prevent mistakes.

First, delete any accounts that you don't actually need. For example, if your company doesn't deal with inventory at all, then you can go ahead and delete the inventory asset account. You are not dealing with it. Make sure you only delete the ones that you definitely do not need. Also, make sure to go through this pruning process before anything is added to the accounts you want to delete. If something is added, this was either a mistake or you may need that account.

Another tip is to make sure that you create parent and child accounts. A parent account is a top-level account. Parent accounts have child accounts under them. So, by assigning a child to a parent account, you create a hierarchy within your chart of accounts. A good example is when you have a parent account for marketing, then your child accounts underneath it might be print marketing, web marketing or SEO marketing. In order to keep clean books, always remember to input expenses into their designated child account. If you paid for an ad in a newspaper, then you would log this in the print marketing account rather than the parent account.

It is always better to keep your chart of accounts simple. The more accounts you have, the more you leave room for error. Using the marketing example again, you wouldn't want to create a ton of child categories unless marketing was a major component of your business. If you are always running ads online, in newspapers and on TV, then you would want to set up this parent/child hierarchy. However, if you pay for a little marketing from time to time (such as when you have sales) then you would be better off only using a single account for marketing. In fact, it might even be better to just include it under your expenses rather than setting up an account. The simpler things are within your chart of accounts, the less likely you are to make mistakes.

Mistake: You Don't Organize Your Items List

We looked at how we create items to sell in chapter four when we looked at the inventory tracking features that QuickBooks uses. We saw how easy it was to create items for sale. But what we didn't touch on was how important it is to keep your items list organized and up to date. As you sell items, you may run out of stock or be selling a limited amount to begin with. When this happens, you should be going through your items list to prune out items that are no longer available. Otherwise, you will notice that your items list starts to become huge even though you only sell a handful of goods at this present moment.

Head on over to your items list and take a look at what you are offering. Are there any items that you no longer sell? If so, you can delete these items using the actions drop-down menu and selecting delete. Double-check that all of the items in your list are correctly labelled. You would be surprised how often an item gets mislabelled because it was entered at the same time as other items were. This is one of those mistakes that can take a while to notice. You charge these items onto invoices and everything is labelled correctly on the invoice. It isn't until you start looking at your inventory stock or your earnings that you notice something odd is happening and you have to track down which item was mislabelled. While you are checking the labels, make sure to check the stock numbers. You may find errors in amounts here and have to add or subtract inventory. If something was incorrectly labelled, then the chances that there are errors with the inventory numbers are that much higher. Finally, make sure that every item is properly priced. If the cost of manufacturing has gone up, so should the cost of your item.

Making sure that your items list is organized and up to date is an important step that many new QuickBooks users fail to take. When you first get started, you will probably only have a few items, and so it won't matter as much if it is messy. But the more items you stock and sell, the more information gets added to your items list and then, before you know it, you find yourself with a messy and confusing list filled with misinformation and items you no longer trade in. Make sure to schedule maintenance on your items list a minimum of once per quarter.

Mistake: You Haven't Set Up Your Preferences

One of the things that many users don't take advantage of is all the settings that QuickBooks offers you. These settings make sure that everything works as you intend it to. A lot of people get into QuickBooks, start using it, and then adapt their bookkeeping system to fit QuickBooks. For example, you may track your dates in a different order than QuickBooks. So now every time you enter a date that looks like 5/7/2019, you have to figure out if that is the 5th of July or the 7th of May. This can be a frustrating experience for you as the main user, but imagine how much worse this is for any accountant that you bring on.

To make things easier, click on the gear on the top menu and open up your settings. Go through the settings and change them as you need to. You can update your email address, change the date settings, and all sorts of other settings that don't particularly change how QuickBooks works but rather alters the aesthetics to easier fit your personal system. This way, when you hand your accountant all the information he needs, he won't spend that extra time sorting through and comparing two different date systems. That means less time spent on your accounts, so less money spent on your accountant.

Mistake: Not Backing Up Your Data

While QuickBooks Online automatically backs up your data using a multi-hard drive approach, it is equally important that you backup your own data. If you are using QuickBooks Desktop instead of QuickBooks Online, then you must do this manually within the application and we'll look at how we do that in one moment. First, let's go over why it is important to backup your own data with QuickBooks Online.

We've seen that every report, invoice or credit memo that we make lets us print them off. This is because it is important to back up your own information. Let's pretend for a moment that you are the only QuickBooks user and something happens to you. Your business is going to need that information, but the only person with the password is now unable to provide it. By keeping a physical backup, you ensure that in the event that something happens to you, your company will be able to rectify any financial issues that are outstanding and continue operating until you are able to return. If you are unable to return, they can use these files to continue in your absence and begin their own accounts. Backing up your data is about security in the event of issues. No one expects something to happen to them, no one expects their company to be hacked. But you backup your data and keep a firewall on your computer to prevent the worst case scenarios.

If you are using QuickBooks Desktop, then you need to back up your digital data as well. You should still keep a physical copy of all your financial data. This is simply good security. But you also are responsible for backing up the digital data that QuickBooks Online handles for its users. You may want to implement a two hard drive system such as Intuit. To backup your data, click on the file option, head down to backup company, and click the create local backup option. You then choose the directory where you wish to save your data. Make sure you know where your data is being kept. If you are using external hard drives, then you will want to clearly label them.

Backing up your data can take some time. But if you implement backing up as a regular part of using QuickBooks, then you will have a much easier time. Instead of leaving your printing for the end of the month, print reports and invoices as soon as you get them. If you make this a part of your QuickBooks routine, then you won't find backing up your data to be so annoying after all.

Chapter Summary

- There are over 270 third party apps which you can connect to your QuickBooks account to really use QuickBooks how you want and to integrate with your other accounts across the net.
- You can find all the information for an app by clicking on the app of your choice while on the apps page within QuickBooks.
- To add a third-party app, click the get app now button and then authorize the app to connect it to your QuickBooks account.
- Keeping your financial data secure is one of QuickBooks' primary concerns.
- QuickBooks makes use of a multi-hard drive backup system, a powerful antivirus service, and a top of the line firewall to prevent hackers. Not only that but they physically back up your information and store it securely off site.
- The ID system you use to create new users also tracks when those users are online, which helps prevent IDs from being compromised and can even help identify where errors were made within QuickBooks.
- It is important that you also take part in the security of your data. Always use secure

networks, firewall, and antivirus software on your work computer.

- It is important to keep your firewall, antivirus software, internet browser, and operating system up to date to ensure the strongest possible protection to keep your financial data secure.
- Errors may happen when you import your banking information to QuickBooks. They are even more likely to happen if you input data by hand.
- You should reconcile your bank and credit card accounts once a month to ensure that everything is up to date and there are no errors.
- Use the reconciling option by clicking on the gear icon on the top menu, selecting reconcile, and then selecting the account you wish to reconcile.
- Compare your bank statement to the transactions listed in reconcile. Select the check mark next to each item as you find it in your statement.
- Once you compare all items and end with a difference balance of $0, you have successful reconciled your account.
- If the difference value is above or below $0, there is an error somewhere which has to be found and identified. The most common

errors are bank service charges, checks that haven't cleared, and transactions you have forgotten to log.

- Keep your chart of accounts organized by deleting any auto-generated accounts which you don't need and by setting up parent and child accounts where appropriate.
- Deleting transactions in QuickBooks is an easy way to mess up your data and create errors down the road in your reporting.
- If you absolutely have to delete a transaction, make sure to spend some time considering what other transactions it is linked to and how you can rectify that information to prevent future errors.
- As your company grows, you will find yourself with a growing and changing list of items you sell. It is important to always keep an organized list of items.
- Delete any items you no longer sell, check the labels of your items and how many you have in stock currently. It is also good to double-check the price.
- You should be updating and cleaning your items list at least once a quarter.
- Click on the gear button at the top of the screen and open your settings. Use these settings to match QuickBooks even closer to your hard copy financial data. This will save

you time sorting your information and your accountant will thank you for it.

- Backing up your data is an important step in keeping your information safe and secure.
- Those using QuickBooks Desktop will need to manually backup their digital data.
- If you print every report and invoice as they are used, you will find physically backing up your data with QuickBooks to be a breeze.

FINAL WORDS

I believe that by now you can see why QuickBooks is such a useful system for small business owners. Because it is so important to keep an accounting system, every business that makes it out there is going to need one. While you can do it by hand, QuickBooks helps by providing a ton of tools to make it easier. It's not just the fact that there are so many tools though, it is that they are gathered together in such an easy-to-use fashion, all under one roof. There are many guides out there on how to do each of these steps yourself, but the speed in which QuickBooks tackles these steps shows that it really does deserve its name. It makes handling your books a quick experience.

The many different plans that QuickBooks offers its users means that you can always pick the bare minimum that you feel would cover your needs. Then, as your company and its accounting needs grow, you can upgrade your QuickBooks plan to get the new features that you require. In this way, QuickBooks will grow alongside your company. QuickBooks is like your accounting toolkit, you add to it as you are faced with new needs. Their tools make sure you can take care of finances quickly, so you can get back to focusing on running your business.

Because QuickBooks lets you set up all the different accounts that you need, it makes a great bookkeeping service. By adding customers and invoicing them directly, you aren't faced with a ton of backout calculations like you would be doing it by hand. That invoice will automatically be calculated against your income and your expenses to be added to your account. You can set up your reports to calculate based on a cash and accrual rate, too. This means that while QuickBooks does the calculations for invoices and what is owed, you can get your reports to show you just the cash that has come through so that you always know the exact dollar value you have to work with at any given time. But if you want to use those calculations, you can always run a report on an accrual basis. Sometimes it can even be beneficial to run a report on both bases for comparison purposes.

A key component of understanding your finances is working with reports and examining where everything rests. Running reports is a great feature and one that is as time consuming as they come. Reports are the cornerstone of your finances since they give you the numbers you need. But getting them means a ton of calculations. You have to go through and find all your income. Add it together to find where you are working from. Then you have to go through your files to find every expense you have accrued during the reporting period. Add those together to get a total. Then you have to subtract the total expenses from the total income. This is the absolute, simplest, most basic report you can run by hand, and even then, it still takes a ton of time to find all the numbers and add them up. QuickBooks almost eliminates this process entirely.

When you first sign up, you are going to have to put in a lot of information by hand. First getting started with QuickBooks doesn't typically feel so quick. But now that you know where to go to enter that information and how to do it, it will be a much quicker experience. Once you have that in place and you begin to use QuickBooks as your primary accounting system, you will be amazed by how many hours you cut out of the bookkeeping and accounting needed for your business. It's not that there's less to do. If anything, I hope that you are now coming to QuickBooks because you are busier than ever. Using all the features that QuickBooks offers is a surefire way to speed up dealing with your finances.

While we covered a ton of features that QuickBooks has, don't forget that Intuit is constantly working on and refining their QuickBooks service. The first version of the QuickBooks software was released way back in 1983 under the name of Quicken. The company has had thirty-six years working on this software. But they aren't done yet. Every year sees new updates and features added. QuickBooks has continued to stay on top of digital business and financial trends. It is this refusal to stop upgrading that makes QuickBooks stand out above many other accounting system options out there. You can be sure that QuickBooks will continue to remain the most commonly suggested bookkeeping and accounting software for small business owners. I certainly recommend it wholeheartedly.

Made in the USA
Middletown, DE
22 April 2020